One Small Step…

![Shell Better Britain Campaign]

SHELL
BETTER
BRITAIN
CAMPAIGN

This publication has been produced with financial support from the Shell Better Britain Campaign. The Campaign, part of Shell UK's community investment programme, has been running for 30 years. It supports community-based action for sustainable development through information, grants and networking.

One small step...

A guide to action on sustainable development in the UK

Edited by
Chris Church and Jan McHarry

COMMUNITY DEVELOPMENT FOUNDATION
• PUBLICATIONS •

First published in 1999 by
The Community Development Foundation
60 Highbury Grove
London N5 2AG

Registered Charity Number 306130

Copyright © Community Development Foundation 1999

Moral rights have been asserted by the editors.

Cataloguing in Publication data
A copy of this record is available from the British Library.

Designed and typeset by Meg Palmer, Third Column
Printed in Great Britain by Crowes Complete Print
Text printed on Sylvancote made from 100% post-consumer waste
Cover printed on Evolve Silk made from 75% post-consumer waste

ISBN 1 901974 16 2

Sustainability demands that we share knowledge and ideas.
We encourage people to reproduce any parts of the text in any appropriate medium, subject to the source – Title, Editors and Publisher – being acknowledged.

Contents

	Page no.
Acknowledgements	vi
Community Development Foundation and SCAN	vii
Using this guide	viii
Introduction – 'only connect'	ix

PART ONE Making things happen: the key issues — 1

1 The local environment — 3
Health and sustainability — 3
Food — 6
Safe environments — 9

2 The wider environment — 3
Biodiversity — 13
Energy use — 16
Sustainable waste management and recycling — 19
Water — 22

3 Getting around — 25
Integrated and sustainable transport — 25

4 Our homes and where we live – the built environment — 29
Sustainable town and cities — 29
Homes and buildings — 31
The open spaces — 32
The neighbourhoods — 32

5 Sustainable livelihoods — 35
Strong and sustainable local economies — 35
Poverty — 38

6 Building stronger communities — 42
Community development — 42
Effective public participation — 44
Towards environmental justice — 46
Access to information — 49

PART TWO The organisations — 53

This section looks at the contributions made to local sustainable development by different groups in society:

The Government	55
Local government	57
Social sector organisations	59
Environment and development non-governmental organisations (NGOs)	60
Community sector organisations	62
Women's organisations	64
Inspiring and enabling young people	66
Educational groups	68
Business	69
Trade unions	73
The arts and local sustainability	74
Religion and faith-based organisations	76

PART THREE Main organisations and contacts — 77

Index of organisations — 84

Acknowledgements

One Small Step… has developed from an original idea to briefly 'map out' the main organisations working on sustainable development in the UK. As this sourcebook shows, the new thinking surrounding sustainability has the potential to touch nearly every part of our lives in the future.

SCAN gratefully acknowledges the support of the Community Development Foundation in the production and distribution of this work and the financial support of the Shell Better Britain Campaign.

Particular thanks for information, direction and help at various stages of this project go to Alison West, the Community Development Foundation, Peter Woodward, Quest Environmental Development Ltd, and Peter Hirst, Community Environment Resource Unit, and Going for Green.

This volume was only made possible thanks to contributions to the text received from the following people and organisations: Richard Armitage; David Birley; Stella Bland; David Boyle; Neil Caldwell; Vicki Carroll; Centre for Creative Communities; Brian Cohen; Amy Cruse; Peter Doran; Margaret Feneley; Vicki Hird; David Lloyd; Kate McLeod; Jane Morris; Nigel Morter; Harry Myers; John Newton; Jane Seymour; Barbara Wilcox.

Additional writing, research and editorial work was by Chris Church and Jan McHarry.

Further material and advice were supplied by Maria Adebowale, Phil Beisley, Simon Brereton, Martin Fodor, Alison Miller, Tim O'Riordan, Paul Slatter, and John Smith and thanks go to Elaine Emling for fact checking and to Catriona May and Jacki Reason for editing.

Many organisations named in the text kindly helped with our enquiries, supplied information and re-checked parts of the text. It has not been possible to credit every piece of information used or drawn upon so this is a collective acknowledgement to those individuals and organisations.

Community Development Foundation

CDF was set up in 1968 to pioneer new forms of community development.

CDF strengthens communities by ensuring the effective participation of people in determining the conditions which affect their lives through:

- influencing policymakers
- promoting best practice
- providing support for community initiatives.

As a leading authority on community development in the UK and Europe, CDF is a non-departmental public body and is supported by the Active Community Unit of the Home Office. It receives substantial backing from local and central government, trusts and business.

CDF promotes community development by enabling people to work in partnership with public authorities, government, business and voluntary organisations to regenerate their communities through:

- local action projects
- conferences and seminars
- consultancies and training programmes
- research and evaluation services
- parliamentary and public policy analysis
- information services
- *CDF News*, a six-monthly newsletter
- publications.

Chairman: Eddie O'Hara, MP
Chief Executive: Alison West

If you would like more details about CDF's work, or a copy or our latest publications catalogue, please contact us at:

Community Development Foundation
60 Highbury Grove
London N5 2AG
Tel: 020 7226 5375
Fax: 020 7704 0313
Email: admin@cdf.org.uk
www.cdf.org.uk

SCAN

One Small Step... has been produced for SCAN, the Sustainable Communities Agencies Network, a loose coalition of a number of national voluntary organisations working on these issues. SCAN recognises that if sustainable development is to move from rhetoric to reality it has to involve people everywhere in working for a better tomorrow – building strong and sustainable communities. SCAN works to link national policies to the people who will be affected by them, and the people who will have to make them work. In a fast-changing and globalising world, strong communities can provide better places to live, and a base from which any group or individual can start to take effective action to put real 'quality' back into their lives.

Using this Guide

This guide aims to help you find the information, contacts and ideas that you need to make your work more effective. It covers a very wide range of issues, simply because work on sustainable development does cover all these issues.

You'll see from the Contents that these sections are further divided, and that each seeks to do three things:

- put the specific topic in a broader context
- identify current issues and concerns
- highlight which organisations are active in this field, and the best sources of information.

Inevitably any such division of topics means that some issues end up in sections that may not be the ones where you expect to find them – consult the Contents list if that's the case. Organisations that are active in several fields are listed under 'Main organisations' beginning on p.79. The Index of Organisations at the end of the book will help you find your way to all the organisations listed in the guide.

This is intended to be a guide and source book rather than a simple directory: for that reason it is more than just names, addresses and websites. We hope that the texts are useful and provide ideas as well as information.

Introduction – 'only connect'

OVER THE LAST FEW YEARS a new concept has caused many people to think hard about their future. Sustainable development has changed from being a new piece of jargon to being a new way of working. All across the UK (and around the world) people are getting to grips with the challenge of creating a more sustainable way of life for themselves and for the communities they live in.

This is a challenge for many reasons. The first challenge is to understand sustainable development. It has been defined in many ways; the original description was of 'development that meets the needs of present generations without compromising the ability of future generations to meet their own needs'. This is fine, but who is to define just what people need?

Most people seem to find it easier to see sustainable development as a way of achieving three objectives – as ensuring that we can:

- protect and improve the **environment**
- ensure **economic** security for everyone
- create a more **equitable** and fairer society.

Integrating these aims will never be easy: many of the major environmental struggles of the last 30 years have been between those seeking to protect the environment and those looking for short-term economic gain. But the idea that we can create a society where we are moving towards these three goals together is a powerful one, and one that is attracting more people and organisations every year.

Working towards sustainable development involves other challenges, of a much more practical nature. If people working on environmental issues want to look at the implications of their work for those working on poverty or health issues, who do they talk to? And how would they start such a dialogue? Are there examples of groups that share quite different short-term objectives working together for longer-term sustainability?

Answering those questions is what this book is all about. All across the UK there are people making links, setting up joint projects, looking at the implications, and trying to turn plans into actions. Here we have tried to identify the key issues for sustainable development and show why these issues matter, who's doing what, and how you can find out more.

There's no doubt that trying to work on projects that link (for instance) transport, health, and economic development will be a challenge. Our educational and professional systems encourage people to specialise in one field: sustainable development means that we have to understand the needs and priorities of people working in several fields, and that we have to try and meet all those needs.

The good news is that, little by little, positive moves towards sustainability are happening. Thousands of organisations are taking small (and not-so-small) steps. There are good ideas and good practice everywhere to learn from and to be inspired by. We hope that this book will help bring many of those small steps together and encourage all those working in the field to make one giant leap towards genuinely sustainable development.

Sustainable development and sustainable communities

There's another big challenge for those working on sustainable development: how to make it real. What does it actually mean on the streets where we live? How do we interest all those people for whom sustainable development is still just a piece of jargon?

Answering these question has led to a lot of work on 'sustainable communities' and the development of new networks and organisations. The Sustainable Communities Agencies Network (SCAN), who have supported the production of this book, links several organisations which work with communities across the UK. They all recognise both that sustainable development is central to their work, and that if the UK is to become more sustainable as a nation, then cities, towns, villages and neighbourhoods all need to take action.

At a local level, sustainable development makes perfect sense. Talk to people anywhere and issues such as energy link to fuel bills and quality of housing; talk about transport and you'll talk about places to park cars, and places for children to play, as well as the state of the bus service.

Bringing all this together is one of the big challenges for all the 'Local Agenda 21' work that has gone on in the UK since 1992. Agenda 21 was the major outcome of the 1992 United Nations 'Earth Summit', which put sustainable development on the political agenda. Agenda 21 is a 40-chapter, 240-page action plan that covers everything from poverty to radioactive wastes, and looks at how all sectors of society have a role to play, and where they should start.

One chapter is on the role of local government, and it calls on local councils everywhere to 'consult with their communities' and to produce their own local version of Agenda 21. Most local councils in the UK have done just that, and there are now hundreds of 'Local Agenda 21' action plans around the UK. Work on those plans has helped people understand both the opportunities and the difficulties that arise from work on sustainable development.

About two-thirds of the action points in Agenda 21 will require some form of local action, but it is important to remember that action by governments is every bit as important. There is little point in a community group working long and hard to improve their neighbourhood if local employers are all closing down or if a new bypass is going to cut straight through their green spaces. It is encouraging that the Government's new Strategy for Sustainable Development includes a section on 'Sustainable Communities'.

The Government also asked SCAN to help identify more pointers to what a 'sustainable community' might actually look like. From this work has come the 'Blueprint for Sustainable Communities', a document that hopes to stimulate more discussion and action by communities and councils.

It's not just governments that affect communities. International organisations such as the World Trade Organisation certainly affect local people, and sometimes it seems as if communities are powerless in this 'globalising' world. Yet just as there are many good examples of communities improving their own circumstances, so there are plenty of examples of groups working together across the world on global issues. Communities often have more power than they realise.

'Sustainable communities' mean different things to different people, from those looking to develop self-sufficient 'eco-villages' to community groups on the poorest housing estates in Britain. SCAN is just one small part of that developing movement, with an approach rooted in community development. Any programme to improve the environment will need to look at the underlying issues, just as any economic programme should also seek to improve the environment and create a better place to live. But for such programmes to work they will need to involve the people they are aiming to help: that is one reason why effective participation is such an important issue for those working on sustainable development.

Part One

*Making things happen:
the key issues*

The local environment

Introduction

WORK ON LOCAL SUSTAINABLE DEVELOPMENT has helped show how our local environment affects us, something that is every bit as important as how we affect our environment. Living in an unsafe and unhealthy environment can lead to ill-health and depression. At the very least it saps energy and creativity from the people who most need to make the changes.

People opposing developments that will affect their local environment have often been described as 'NIMBYs' (Not In My Back Yard), but if we don't care about our back yard then who will? The challenge that sustainable development gives us is to recognise that the area we have to care for may indeed start with our back yards, but stretches out across the Earth.

'If the council can't deal with the dog-mess, how's it ever going to do anything about this global warming business?'

Hackney resident, 1996

It's a sad fact that 'troubles seldom come singly'. Poorest communities often have to suffer the worst environments, and consistently face high crime rates. Poor environmental quality means all sorts of things: poor and hard-to-heat housing, high levels of air pollution and traffic, shortage of green space and play space, unsafe streets and often a lack of support for people who do want to do something about it. Litter and dog fouling make the area look and feel even worse. Link all that with a lack of money and it's not surprising that many people become alienated and resentful, even apathetic.

This first section looks at three areas:

- health
- food
- safety.

Good health, a decent diet, and a safe place to live are fundamentals that many people take for granted, yet for many they are big problems. If someone doesn't have these fundamentals, it's not surprising if they don't get involved in environmental improvement work.

'If you ain't got your health, you ain't got nothing.'

Another Hackney resident, 1997

Health and sustainability

Agenda 21 clearly states that 'sound development is not possible without a healthy population'. Development activities affect the environment in a way that can cause or exacerbate health problems. At the same time, a lack of development can adversely affect the health of many people.

Proposals within Agenda 21 focus on:

- meeting primary health care needs
- controlling communicable diseases
- coping with urban health problems
- reducing health risks from environmental pollution
- protecting vulnerable groups such as infants, women, indigenous groups and very poor people.

These are not new issues: the Chartered Institute of Environmental Health Officers (CIEH), the main professional organisation in the field, was formed by workers in the nineteenth century facing just these issues.

KEY LINKAGES:

Other relevant sections of this guide are: Transport, Housing, Poverty, Strong communities

A new common agenda

For many years environment and health agendas were seen as separate, but now there is a realisation that it makes sense to tackle environment and health issues together. A new public health agenda is emerging, addressing the links between environmental quality and health, tackled within the context of both the national sustainable development strategy and the 'Health of the Nation' programme. The 1999 World Health Organisation European Ministerial Conference on Environment and Health also provided new ideas and guidance.

Action on health can be divided into three broad areas:

- enabling people to develop and maintain their health on a day-to-day basis through individual and community action;
- preventing people from becoming ill by regulating hazards and providing information on risks;
- treating them when they are ill or injured, including support to manage their illness.

Traditionally, the National Health Service (NHS) has focused on provision of treatment with some resourcing going towards prevention issues. Although the first issue – health promotion – has been addressed by a variety of Government departments (including education, environment and social security) there has been little real co-ordination. Ensuring the long-term viability of the NHS requires a multi-faceted approach, building on technological advances in the treatment of illness but also investing in the long-term health of the population so they are less likely to become ill.

The government's White Paper 'Saving Lives – Our Healthier Nation' 1999 identified four key 'illness' areas – heart and circulatory disease, cancer, mental illness and accidents – for reduction. It also identified three 'settings' – Healthy Schools, Healthy Workplaces, and Healthy Neighbourhoods – as ways of developing and maintaining health. These initiatives link directly with the framework of Health 21 and Agenda 21.

Health 21 is a new WHO framework which updates the 'Health for All 2000' principles, and reflects the importance of co-ordinating activity with reference to Agenda 21. The 21 targets include: health of young people and infants; healthy ageing; improving mental health; reducing communicable and non-communicable diseases; reducing injury from violence and accidents; promoting a healthy and safe physical environment; reducing harm from tobacco, alcohol, drugs; multi-sectoral responsibility for health; managing for quality of care; and policies and strategies for health for all.

In addition, any government seeking economic sustainability has to balance the needs of the currently productive part of the population with those who have already made their contribution and those who will become productive in the future.

Because of the strong links between Agenda 21 and Health 21, it has been suggested that it would be most appropriate to use both frameworks to balance the needs of people and the environment in the search for sustainable health. The Health 21 target – mobilising partners for health – is extremely relevant to this process.

A more sustainable health service

To improve the health service we need to make the health system more sustainable, and reduce the environmental impact of its activities. This can be done in various ways:

- ensure that the treatment of illness and injury is carried out in as sustainable a way as possible, e.g. careful purchasing and sourcing of materials, energy sources and efficiency measures;
- reduce the use of treatment services by ensuring that access to appropriate information about risks of illness and injury is made available through as many channels as possible;
- reduce the use of treatment services by ensuring that individuals, households and communities have the opportunity to shape a safe and healthy physical and social environment;
- plan health services, hospitals and other centres to improve their environmental performance.

One example of such an approach is the Healthy Transport toolkit launched by the pressure group Transport 2000 with support from the Health Education Authority. This is a practical guide for hospital managers which picks up on points reflected in the Government's White Paper 'The Future of Transport' (1998) suggesting the need for hospitals to produce green transport plans.

NHS Estates, part of the Department of Health, also have an environment policy manager who can provide advice. Pinderfields Hospitals NHS Trust recently achieved a 34% reduction in energy use – equivalent to saving £370,000 annually. Background material for the Government's Sustainable Development Strategy includes a guidance note on the implications for the health sector.

The development of a truly sustainable health service is clearly a considerable challenge. There is no finite limit to the development of treatments or to illnesses and injuries requiring attention. Whilst many people in the world do not have access to basic primary care (a family doctor or nurse), the combination of modern technologies are delivering more specific treatments to more specific ailments.

This exponential growth in the treatment of illness and injury at an individual level tends to mask the essentially unequal distribution of health resources (which is no different from other global or national inequalities).

Local action

The government is clear that local action is required to address national inequalities in health. Hospital care is expensive and often 'high tech', while there is much that can be achieved locally to maintain health and reduce risks of illness and injury. Opportunities to develop 'sustainable health' include:

- *Healthy Living Centres* – a £300 million UK-wide initiative funded by the New Opportunities Fund to generate improvements in health in areas of greatest need;
- *Healthy Neighbourhoods* – can be seen as the context for Healthy Schools and Workplaces, providing a framework for action which could include transport, food sourcing and delivery and action to enhance social cohesion;
- *Primary Care Groups* – a restructuring of 'frontline' health care which includes responsibility for health improvement.

Other initiatives include Health Action Zones and specific action on smoking. There is also a need to focus on links between social exclusion, health, and poverty. The Public Health Alliance have been running a project on poverty and health for some years and are now looking at how this may link with sustainability issues.

The increasing integration of such policy areas can be seen in the Healthy Cities Movement. This WHO programme links hundreds of cities around the world, and a growing number in the UK. Healthy Cities is now directly linked to the European Sustainable Cities and Towns Campaign, and have produced joint materials.

Key organisations

Community participation is the key to many of these new initiatives. As yet there are no clear patterns emerging of how partnerships will develop. The ideal model is where local authorities, health authorities, voluntary and private agencies and local communities develop/negotiate 'win-win' partnerships where health, environmental protection and economic interests are balanced to achieve sustainable development.

The reality will probably be a few highly developed and full partnerships with a larger number of less coherent examples. Because viable partnerships and community participation takes time and resources to develop, the whole process is unlikely to deliver nationwide standards quickly. All these initiatives are currently under development and with so many elements being 'joined up', any one of them could influence progress of the whole new health agenda.

Health & Housing
Room 65, London Fruit Exchange, Brushfield Street, London E1 6EP
Tel: 020 7375 3553 Fax: 020 7375 0577
Email: info@healthousing.org.uk

H&H promotes awareness of the connection between good housing and good health through research and training.

Health for All Network (UK)
PO Box 101, Liverpool, L69 5BE Tel: 0151 207 0919 (Elaine Mooney) Email: ukhfan@livjm.ac.uk.

The Health for All Network (HFAN) is an internationally-recognised structure that enables those working within the key principles of equity, community participation and intersectoral collaboration to meet and share information, research and experiences.

NHS Executive
All inquiries to: NHS Executive, Quarry House, Quarry Hills, Leeds LS2 7UE Tel: 0113 254 5000

The NHS Executive is responsible for all aspects of development of the NHS. They have recently set up a useful Health Action Zones website and information service at www. haznet.org.uk

The Pioneer Health Centre
Healthy Living Project, 259 Stainbeck Road, Leeds, LS7 3PR Tel: 0113 225 0952
Email: hlproject@dial.pipex.com

The PHC is a charity and member of the Health for All Network (UK) which promotes the integration of local health, leisure, social and environmental activity to achieve community well being. The charity is now managing The Healthy Living Project which will support communication and information sharing between Healthy Living initiatives funded by the New Opportunities Fund.

Primary Care Groups and Healthy Neighbourhoods
Contact your local Health Authority to obtain local information. The final 'Our Healthier Nation' White Paper is now available. Details of how to apply for Healthy Living Centres funding from the New Opportunities Fund are available from www.nof.org.uk

UK Public Health Association (UKPHA)
138 Digbeth, Birmingham B5 6DR Tel: 0121 678 8842
Fax: 0121 643 4541 Email: pha@online.co.uk

UKPHA was launched in March 1999 and has developed out of the merger of the Public Health Alliance and the Association for Public Health. It runs a wide range of programmes, and has health and sustainability as a key principle in its work.

Further information

Publications

Green Gym Best Practice Guide – A publication on how to combine nature conservation and health development. Available from British Trust for Conservation Volunteers BTCV Tel: 01403 730572
Email South@btcv.org.uk

Growing Places for Life – a study of local projects in England and the potential to link action to benefit people and the environment. Available from The Healthy Living Project (see above)

Healthy Living Centres – Bringing together Health for All and Agenda 21 – A report of a seminar held in Leeds, April 1998 is available for £6 from Health for All (see above).

The Healthy Transport Toolkit – The Health Education Authority, in collaboration with Transport 2000, has published a guide for developing more sustainable transport for hospitals and health care professionals. Contact Transport 2000, 12–18 Hoxton St, London N1 6NG Tel: 0207 613 0743 (Orders preferred in writing via Fax: 0207 613 5280). Price £20.

Sustainable Development & Health: concepts principles and frameworks for action for European cities and towns. 1997, WHO.

Websites

HLNET – the electronic discussion list for Healthy Living Centres provides a means of linking projects across the UK. For details on how to join please contact The Healthy Living Project Email: hlproject@dial.pipex.com

The World Health Organisation website – www.who.dk is a good source of health related information on many topics including Healthy Cities and also the Verona Initiative which offers a benchmarking framework for local action.

● Food

Food is central to everyone's lives, has a major impact on environmental and human health and plays a significant part in the UK economy and trade. Recent food crises and the current debate over genetically modified organisms, heightened by recent publicity and consumer pressure, have all helped put food high on the political agenda. As a result interest in sustainable agriculture and safe food has grown very fast amongst the public.

Chapter 14 of Agenda 21 emphasises the need for sustainable agriculture and rural development and calls for measures to ensure access to nutritionally adequate food, employment to alleviate poverty, and natural resource management. In 1997 'Earth Summit II' called for 'continued efforts for the eradication of poverty through capacity building to reinforce local food systems'.

The UK Government's Sustainable Development Strategy calls for 'a new approach to foster dialogue between consumers and producers to find practical solutions to consumer concerns'. Many Agenda 21 groups find that working on food issues is an ideal way to both assess sustainability in their area and also to engage the local community in looking at problems and, more importantly, the solutions. 'Food has the potential to educate people about sustainability, support sustainable production, help in the regeneration of local communities, and link action on health, poverty and the environment.' Government health policy attaches increasing importance to diet and nutrition in maintaining people's health – 'A good diet is an important way of protecting health ... research suggests that a third of all cancers are the result of a poor diet' (*Our Healthier Nation*, 1998).

KEY LINKAGES:
Other relevant sections of the Guide are:
Health, Biodiversity, Built environment, Poverty

Current issues and activities

Four key areas dominate activities on food in the UK, namely:

- CAP reform and World Trade Organisation negotiations;
- food safety including genetic engineering in food production, BSE and the emerging Food Standards Agency;
- animal welfare;
- environmental damage such as loss of biodiversity and chemical use.

CAP reform

Reform of the European Common Agricultural Policy (CAP) is central to any long-term attempt to create a more sustainable farming system in Europe. Recent official reform proposals include more support for ecological farming, as well as major changes to the management of Structural Funding which provides aid to rural areas.

UK organisations including SUSTAIN, the Royal Society for the Protection of Birds (RSPB), National Consumer Council, Compassion in World Farming (CIWF) and Catholic Institute for International Relations believe that more radical reforms in all sectors, particularly the arable, are badly needed. They are running a campaign to highlight the many flaws in the CAP and the Agriculture Agreement of the GATT and to show just how the environment, animals, consumers, the developing world and the economy suffer from a completely inefficient and ineffective trade policy. Recommendations include an urgent phase-out of export subsidies and a switch from supporting farmers world-wide for production to supporting good practice and enhanced production methods, beneficial to the environment and animal welfare. Many groups are also concerned about how far international negotiations on trade and agriculture may also influence future reforms.

GMOs

The dominant feature of food reporting in the media is on genetic engineering. Public concern has grown rapidly over the effects of introducing new genes into food, the direct and indirect effects on the environment and the potential health impacts on humans and animals. Soya is the main product being currently traded from the US and GE soya (herbicide resistant) products are available now in UK stores, although consumer pressure has been successful in getting many supermarket chains and other stores to stop stocking products containing GM foodstuffs. New regulations will mean that every restaurant has to identify GM foods on their menus.

Friends of the Earth, GenetiX and direct action groups are allocating considerable resources to exposing the existing GE crop sites, providing information for the public and decision-makers and lobbying government and industry to bring in a moratorium or ban on the growing and consumption of GE foods in the

UK and elsewhere. Third World development groups are also becoming more concerned about the impact of GE technology, for instance on farmers' ability to protect their crops and to sow farm-saved seeds.

The various industry bodies promoting genetic engineering are also promoting their side of the debate. The Food and Drink Federation are running a 'Food Futures' programme and have produced a range of materials on the subject, and their website has links to other relevant bodies.

The Food Standards Agency

In response to the BSE crisis and other food issues the Government announced the formation of a new Food Standards Agency. They put in place a comprehensive consultation exercise and groups across the whole interest spectrum responded. SUSTAIN is co-ordinating groups' responses to the proposed remit of the new FSA. A major disappointment is that responsibility for pesticides and veterinary products will remain with MAFF.

Cruelty-free food

Animal welfare issues lie at the heart of many people's concerns about food. However, the sales of free range eggs, whilst increasing, are still small. Groups such as Compassion in World Farming are working to educate not only the general public but also retailers and processors (e.g. commercial cake makers) of the benefits of free range and organic farming. They are also lobbying for an end to battery farming, genetic engineering in animal farming, live animal exports (some of which are currently supported by taxpayers' subsidies), and policies which exacerbate welfare problems such as the CAP. A recent Europe-wide ban (from 2012) on battery hen cages for egg layers is a recent victory.

Chemical use

Between 1950 and 1985 there was a five-fold increase in the use of chemical fertilisers, and a 32-fold increase in the use of pesticides and herbicides world-wide. In the UK farmers use 29.2 million kg of pesticides (active ingredient) annually. The direct cost of that chemical load is hard to assess but includes removal of chemicals from drinking water, the cost of lost biodiversity such as birds and wild plants, and the cost of healthcare for those poisoned by farm chemicals and pharmaceuticals.

There are also increasing scientific concerns about the real safety of many chemicals when combined – the 'cocktail' effect – and the potential hazards for children, before and after birth.

Other related food and agriculture topics rising up the agenda include: the damage caused by out-of-town superstores to the environment and farmer income; the high street and society; 'food miles' and the impact of long-distance food transport; food poverty in the UK and world-wide, and fair/ethical trading issues.

Local action

Anyone with a garden can start action locally, by growing more of their own food. Allotments are also available in many towns and cities although in some areas they are under pressure from development. City farms and community gardens are also good places to start for anyone seeking to 'grow local'.

New reports have shown just how much food is being grown in urban areas, and there is much that can be done to support communities wishing to grow food. Food growing projects can also strengthen communities by involving people in practical projects: several good ethnic minority environmental projects have started in this way. Food projects can also help improve people's physical and mental health and can help tackle problems of organic waste disposal.

Another way in which people are taking action is to 'buy organic'. Organic produce is grown in ways which protect animal welfare and the environment, without artificial biocides and fertilisers. The rapid rise in sales is testament to the public concern over the possible impact on health of these chemicals – demand rose by over 40% in one month in 1999! Unfortunately 70% of organic produce sold in the UK is imported meaning lost benefits to UK farmers and more food miles.

Getting fresh and organic food can sometimes be difficult. One way which people can support local food production is to set up and support 'farmers markets'. This idea has come from the USA where in many cities local farmers and food producers set up in a market or public space once a week and sell their produce direct to the public. Local authorities can do a great deal to help such markets start up. Organic food is also being delivered to people's doors by an increasing number of 'box schemes' where members pay a regular fee for a box of fresh fruit and vegetables once a week.

Organic food is still expensive and for the poorest people it can be out of the question. And it's not just organic foods – some poorer areas have become 'food deserts' with only limited shopping facilities selling a narrow range of foods. Anti-poverty workers are now increasingly focusing on helping poor communities have better food through projects such as community cafes, food co-ops etc.

Key organisations

Allotments Coalition Trust (ACT)
111 Magdalen Road, Oxford OX4 Tel: 01865 72 2016

The ACT is being set up for the protection and promotion of allotments.

Compassion in World Farming (CIWF)
5 Charles Street, Petersfield, Hants GU32 3 EH
Tel. 01730 26 4208/26 8863 Fax: 01730 26 0791
Email: compassion@ciwf.co.uk Website: www.ciwf.co.uk

CIWF work to improve welfare standards for farm animals and stop the live export trade.

Farmers Market Help-Line
Tel: 01225 891422

This help-line (currently only staffed part-time) helps put producers and markets in touch, advise, and is looking into accreditation. They are also developing a website, research and training packages. For a full list of UK markets send an SAE to Local Food Links at the Soil Association (below).

Federation of City Farms and Community Gardens (FCFG)
The Green House, Hereford St, Bedminster, Bristol BS3 4NA Tel: 0117 923 1800 Fax: 0117 923 1900
Email: farmgarden@btinternet.com

FCFG promotes and supports city farming and gardening. It produces a range of advice materials. Membership is open to any community-managed project.

Food and Drink Federation
6 Catherine Street, London WC2B 5JJ
Tel: 0207 836 2460 Website: www.foodfuture.org.uk

The FDF run a 'Food Futures' campaign and have produced a booklet on 'GM Foods: the benefits and risks'.

Friends of the Earth
(see Main organisations)

Campaigns for the environment and sustainable development. Has a Campaign for Real Food and works specifically on genetically engineered food issues. FoE Cymru in Wales and FoE Scotland also work on food and related issues.

Health Education Authority
Trevelyan House, 30 Great Peter St, London SW1P 2HW
Tel: 020 7413 2033

Food and Low Income Database link to CAN site. The HEA is developing a food and low-income database in collaboration with Sustain, and is part of the Food Poverty Network. The database can help make contacts, plan a needs assessment, and exchange information and expertise. New projects can be registered on the database.
Website: www.food.poverty.hea.org.uk .

Henry Doubleday Research Association (HDRA)
Ryton Organic Gardens, Coventry CV8 3LG
Tel: 01203 303517 Fax: 01203 639229
Website: www.hdra.org

HDRA promote and research organic gardening and food production.

Permaculture Association
BCM Permaculture Association, London WC1N 3XX
Tel/Fax: 070411 39 0170
Email: office@permaculture.org.uk
Website: www.permaculture.org.uk

The Association promotes sustainable growing and living through networking, research, and training.

Pesticides Trust
Eurolink Centre, 49 Effra Road, London SW2 1BZ
Tel: 0171 274 8895 Fax: 0171 274 9084
Email: pesttrust@gn.apc.org
Website: www.gn.apc.org/pesticidestrust

The Trust is an independent charity addressing the health and environmental problems of pesticides and working for a sustainable future.

RSPB
(see Biodiversity)

RSPB also campaigns to reform agriculture policy and promote more sustainable food systems.

Soil Association
86 Colston St, Bristol BS1 5BB Tel: 0117 929 0661
Fax: 0117 925 2504 Website: www.soilassociation.org

The Association works on organic research, promotion and certification, and runs local food links projects, farmers' markets and campaigns on GMOs.

SUSTAIN – the Alliance for Better Food and Farming
White Lion St, London N1 Tel: 0171 837 1228
Fax: 0171 837 1141 Email: sustaina@charity.vfree.com
Website: www.users.charity.vfree.com/s/sustain

The Alliance has a combined membership of 105 organisations who are solely or partly concerned with improving the food system in the UK, Europe and world-wide. They include farmer, organic, consumer, health, welfare, environment, development, and education groups. The Alliance works to co-ordinate lobbying and information campaigns, runs key projects to show how the food system can be more sustainable.

Further information

Publications

City Harvest: the feasibility of growing more food in London, SUSTAIN, 1999

Factory Farming and the myth of cheap food, CIWF, 1997

The Food Magazine – regular subscription magazine on food issues by the Food Commission, 94 White Lion Street, London N1 9PF.

The Food Miles Report – the dangers of long distance food transport, 1998, SAFE Alliance, London. Update and Food Miles Action Pack 1996, SAFE, London

Growing Food in Cities, SAFE/NFA, 1997

The Living Land, Jules Pretty, Earthscan, London 1998

Local Harvest, Kate de Selincourt, London, Lawrence & Wishart, 1997

MAFF, *Agriculture in the UK* – annual reports. HMSO, London 1996

The Organic Directory 1999–2000 edition. Compiled by Clive Litchfield, Green Earth Books, 1998. 192pp. ISBN 1-900322-09-9. Where to get hold of organic produce in England, Scotland, Wales & Channel Islands. The directory lists retailers, producers, wholesalers and manufacturers, in addition to suppliers of organic gardening materials, farm gate sales and shops, local 'veg' box schemes plus a further reference/information section.

Pesticide News – regular publication by the Pesticides Trust, London.

Permaculture Magazine – available quarterly, on subscription, from Permanent Publications, Hyden House Ltd, The Sustainability Centre, East Meon, Hampshire GU32 1HR. Tel: 01730 82 3311 Fax: 01730 82 3322. Email: hello@permaculure.co.uk Website: http://www.permaculture.co.uk

Soil Association quarterly journal *'Organic Farming'* available on subscription, details SAE 40–56 Victoria Street, Bristol BS1 6BY.

Splice of Life – regular subscription publication from Genetics Forum, London (address)

Sustainable Agriculture and Food – Local Agenda 21 Roundtable Guidance note, 1998, available from the IDA (see MOL)

Websites

www.foe.co.uk – Friends of the Earth – lots of info about GMOs

www.oneworld.org/tlio – This Land Is Ours – campaign for land reform

www.netlink.co.uk/users/abracad/orground.html – an organic box scheme website

www.hdra.org.uk – The HDRA organic growing group's website

www.maff.gov.uk – the MAFF website

● Safe environments

Community safety and sustainable development

The concept of *community safety* was developed in the early 1980s. It marked a departure from earlier approaches to crime prevention which had focused primarily on detection and deterrence by the police and on the physical security of property. Community safety represents a wider approach. It addresses fear of crime and the particular crime threats faced by women and by people from minorities. It considers causes of crime as well as preventive measures, and critically, it seeks to involve local authorities, voluntary and community groups and commercial organisations as well as the police.

The earliest community safety initiatives were implemented on high crime housing estates in the mid-1980s. Now, under the *Crime and Disorder Act* 1998, local councils and the police have a duty to carry out a local audit of crime problems and to prepare a community safety strategy for the whole area.

The importance of community safety in the achievement of sustainable communities is well recognised. When the UK's Local Agenda 21 Steering Group adopted 13 themes for sustainable development, its ninth theme was that:

> *'A sustainable community would be one in which people live without fear of crime, or persecution on account of their race, gender, sexuality or beliefs.'*
>
> **Local Government Management Board**, 1995

KEY LINKAGES:
Other relevant sections of the guide are:
Built environment, Community development

Crime problems in England and Wales

So how much crime is there and who is most affected by it? Not all crime is reported to the police, not all reported crime is officially recorded, and recording practices have not always been consistent, so making judgements about trends has been problematic. In 1981 the Home Office initiated the British Crime Survey. The survey, undertaken every two to three years, measures crime against people living in households (the crimes which most affect most people – vandalism, burglary, vehicle related theft, cycle theft, other household theft, personal theft, robbery, wounding, common assault).

The latest British Crime Survey (BCS) estimates that there were nearly 16.5 million crimes in 1997, a fall of 14% since the previous survey in 1995. However, even with the trend of rising crime apparently reversed, the 1997 survey still counted 49% more crime than the first in 1981. 1 in 3 people were the victims of one or more crimes in 1997, almost two-thirds of which were property-related. Crimes of violence resulting in injury were much rarer.

Burglary

In 1997 on average just under 1 in every 18 households was burgled at least once. However the rate was twice as high where the head of household was:

- unemployed or
- a single parent or
- aged 16–24.

Burglary was also above average:

- in areas with high levels of *physical disorder* such as vandalism, graffiti and fly-tipping;
- in inner city areas;
- on council estates; and
- where household income is very low.

Violent crime

There is less risk of being a victim of violent crime than burglary. In 1997, 1 in 21 adults were the victims of some type of violent crime (wounding, common assault, robbery or snatch theft), although a small proportion of these offences resulted in bodily injury. Being unemployed, a single parent, on low income, or a young adult significantly increases the risk of victimisation. The biggest single risk factor is being a young adult male. 21% of men aged 16–24 were victims of violence in 1997. Young women also experience more than average violent crime. By contrast less than 1% of women aged 65–74 experienced violence and only 0.2% of those aged 75+.

Of the 3.3 million crimes of violence in 1997, 2.3 million were categorised as domestic. Violence by strangers is much less common.

Fear of crime

The 1995 British Crime Survey found that over 20% of adults were very worried about burglary, mugging and car crime. A third of women were very worried about rape. Nearly half of women said they felt unsafe walking alone in their area after dark. For elderly women the figure is 60%.

The BCS usefully points out that by and large fear is not irrational. Those most fearful of crime tend to live in areas where crime is greatest, and also to have the least resources for coping with being a victim, e.g. frailty, poor health, low income, low or no insurance, inability to move to a safer area.

3% of women and 1% of men stay at home all the time in part because of concern about crime; in poorer areas, the figures are higher. However, much larger proportions of people surveyed took other precautions outside the home to avoid street crime. 25% said that they had changed where they went or what they did in the past couple of years. 14% said they avoided particular locations and events; nearly half of women make sure they go out at night with someone else.

The picture in the BCS is echoed by many smaller scale surveys on crime and community safety. It shows that on the one hand

- crime has fallen slightly in recent years;
- violent crime resulting in serious injury is very rare.

On the other hand

- there is still 50% more crime now than 20 years ago;
- poor people living in the poorest areas and on housing estates are most likely to be victims of crime;
- people most fearful of crime are those with most to be concerned about.

Strategic approaches to community safety

The first community safety initiatives tended to focus on a single area or theme: a housing estate with serious crime problems; or elderly people in a locality at risk of burglary. More recently, as with other LA21 concerns such as waste and transport, the importance of strategies for community safety across and throughout a local council area has been recognised.

From the late 1980s increasing numbers of councils, in partnership with the police and other bodies, began to develop co-ordinated, strategic approaches to crime problems. Then in 1998, the *Crime and Disorder Act* placed a duty on all local councils and the police to work together with other local agencies to analyse local crime problems, to develop strategies to tackle them, and to subject the strategy to widespread public consultation.

The content of local strategies will depend on the analysis of local problems and on the resources available locally and nationally to implement the strategies. Indeed each strategy is likely to be made up of:

- existing initiatives with some improved co-ordination or coverage;
- new management initiatives with only marginal costs;
- the inclusion of community safety objectives in other capital programmes;
- the use of government grants and SRB schemes for specific community safety and crime prevention projects;
- voluntary and community sector initiatives only partially dependent on government funding.

The range of initiatives within a local strategy might well include:

- environmental measures to enhance safety on housing estates, town centres and in other high crime areas. These include design and planning guidance for architects and developers; better management of public areas with particular attention to landscaping and to litter, fly-tipping, graffiti etc.; introduction of phone entry, concierge, enhanced door security etc.; improved lighting; the creation of safe pedestrian routes, the creation of safer public transport; CCTV schemes in town centres etc.;
- preventive measures to reduce the chances of young people getting involved in serious offending and being victims of crime including health and education support for pre-school children and their families; the creation of safe play areas; work in schools to reduce truancy and to deal with disruptive behaviour without exclusion; developing more attractive leisure and training opportunities for young people;
- development of comprehensive advice, treatment and harm reduction initiatives to counter drug and alcohol abuse;
- protection and support for the victims of crime, particularly elderly people and victims of racial or domestic violence and abuse, together with more responsive initiatives to tackle nuisance neighbours;
- capacity building initiatives to improve the quality and impact of local community projects by enhancing the skills of those who run them;
- anti-poverty, education and other measures to counter social exclusion;
- co-ordination and promotion of initiatives to the wider public.

Of course, many of the individual projects and initiatives making up a community safety strategy are not new. What is new is the focus on management, service delivery, co-ordination, evaluation and monitoring.

Community safety and Local Agenda 21

Community safety is part of sustainable development. The local strategic approach to the delivery of community safety in many ways mirrors the local sustainable development strategy envisaged under LA21. But of course there are other linkages. Many community safety initiatives can contribute to other sustainable development objectives. Some community safety initiatives may well have other positive environmental outcomes. The following examples are drawn from established community safety initiatives:

- The creation of safe pedestrian routes and safer public transport have been focuses for some community safety strategies. They contribute to the development of mobility not dependent on the car. For poorer people who do not have access to a car, safe transport may be the difference between taking part in community activity and staying in.
- In many areas tackling litter and fly tipping has been a priority. Besides reducing physical disorder, such measures also link with good sustainable waste management practice.
- Initiatives aimed at diverting young people in run-down areas away from offending behaviour increasingly include practical environmental and conservation components, from managing local wooded areas to drama workshops on environmental issues to designing and building play space for younger children for example.
- Several town centres have CCTV and town centre management initiatives which are aimed at creating safer, pleasanter environments for local residents and traders. Here, community safety improvements help to protect and sustain the local economy and to counter the trend to out-of-town car dependent shopping.
- Planting, landscaping, lighting and security design are increasingly sophisticated, achieving a balance between security, appearance, environmental quality and impact.

There can be conflicts: on one estate, some residents wanted an old woodland removed so that children could play on an adjacent field in full view of their parents. On another, the use of paths and routes both by young cyclists and by elderly residents was contested. But usually the strategic approach to community safety is entirely consistent with the sustainable development principles of LA21. Conflicts between security and environmental objectives can also be minimised by ensuring LA21 input into the development of a community safety strategy.

It is important therefore that community safety is recognised as a key component in sustainable development. Those concerned with developing local sustainable development strategies under LA21 must involve themselves as fully as possible in the development of community safety locally. Where possible, LA 21 interests should be represented on local bodies set up to oversee community safety strategy.

Key organisations

Local authority crime audits and community safety strategies

All local councils and the police have a duty to prepare audits of local crime problems and strategies to tackle them. This process is designed to be one of partnership and to involve voluntary and community bodies as well as statutory agencies. For further information on local community safety strategy contact the local police crime prevention officer or the council community safety officer or chief executive's department.

Government crime prevention policy is developed by the:

Crime Reduction Unit
Home Office, 50 Queen Anne's Gate, London SW1H 9AT Tel: 0207 273 4000 Fax: 0207 271 8334

Community safety organisations

Several nationally-based voluntary sector bodies develop projects and undertake research into effective community safety initiatives. These include:

SNU (Safe Neighbourhoods Unit)
16 Winchester Walk, London SE1 9AG
Tel: 020 7403 6050 Fax: 020 7403 8060
Email: SNU@SNU-1.demon.co.uk

Crime Concern
Signal Point, Station Road, Swindon, Wilts. SN1 1FE
Tel: 01793 514596 Fax: 01793 514654

NACRO (National Alliance for the Care and Resettlement of Offenders)
169 Clapham Road, London SW9 0PU
Tel: 020 7582 6500 Fax: 020 7735 4666

All these organisations work with communities; Crime Concern also has a specialist Youth Unit, and NACRO works with offenders and those at risk.

Further information

Publications

The 1998 British Crime Survey, Catriona Mirlees-Black, Tracey Budd, Sarah Partridge and Pat Mayhew (1998), London Home Office Research, Development and Statistics Directorate – Statistics about crime.

Crime the Local Solution: Current practice case studies and local initiatives for community safety, Steve Osborn and Henry Shaftoe, 1997, London, Local Government Management Board

Design for Secure Residential Environments, Steve Crouch, Henry Shaftoe and Roy Fleming (1999), London, Longmans

Reducing Offending – Ways of dealing with offending behaviour, Christopher Nuttall (editor), 1998, London, Home Office Research and Statistics Directorate

Safer neighbourhoods? Successes and failures in crime prevention, Steve Osborn and Henry Shaftoe, 1995, London, SNU and Joseph Rowntree Foundation

Turning the tide: crime, community and prevention, Jon Bright, 1997, London, Demos

Websites

Community Safety – The first British website on community safety was established at the University of West of England, Bristol: www-fbe.uwe.ac.uk/commsafe/commsafe.htm

2 The wider environment

Introduction

FEW GOVERNMENTS WOULD HAVE TURNED UP to the 1992 UN Summit if it had been about the state of the streets. World leaders went to Rio because the facts and figures make one thing very clear: our planetary environment is in a mess.

The figures are brutally clear: species of plants and animals are becoming extinct 1000 times more rapidly than they would through natural evolution; the hole in the ozone layer has grown alarmingly over the last fifteen years; the average temperature is creeping upwards and the signs of global climate change become clearer every year; and while all this is going on over one billion people still lack access to safe drinking water.

It is undeniable that most of these problems are due to our own activities, and are the results of meeting not just our needs but also our desires. The bottom line is, as Agenda 21 said, that 'the major cause of the continued deterioration of the global environment is the unsustainable pattern of consumption and production, particularly in industrialised countries'. Tackling consumption head-on will be difficult, but there are a great many ways we can start.

In the early 1990s it was widely said that saving the planet was up to all of us, and that simple actions could solve the problems. The 'green consumer boom' fuelled the idea that somehow, if we all only bought the right CFC-free aerosol, everything would be alright … Of course, it's not that easy: recycling may make sense, but only if there is a market for all that separated material. Leaving the car at home is not easy for people with children living in areas with no buses.

The bottom line is that individual action and behaviour change is vital, but it must be backed up by community, city, and government-level action. The good news is that there is an enormous amount of activity developing at city and community level that can help turn international environmental policy into meaningful action on the ground.

● Biodiversity

'Praise be, my Lord, for our sister,
Mother Earth, who sustains and governs us
And brings forth diverse fruits
with many hued flowers and grasses.'

St Francis

The world includes a vast diversity of plants, animals and other life forms. None of these organisms can exist without others to support them. The concept of the food-chain is familiar to most people, but in reality the web of interactions between plants, animals and their environment is far more complex. Humankind is part of this web and is affected by any upset in the balance as much as any other organism.

This biological diversity exists in terms of species, in the genetic variety within species, and within ecosystems. It is the stuff of life, it makes the planet what it is. It is the planet's biodiversity. A formal definition of biodiversity is:

'The richness and variety of plants, birds, animals and insects that exist throughout the world.'

Making Biodiversity Happen, DETR 1998

Humanity depends on this biodiversity in all sorts of ways, for:

- pleasure – e.g. aesthetics, gardening, bird watching, tourism
- variety of place – e.g. local distinctiveness
- food varieties
- drugs and remedies – e.g. aspirin is derived originally from the bark of willow trees and from meadowsweet
- building materials – e.g. timber.

Biodiversity is essential to maintain our standard of living, quality of life, and indeed our lives. It is our life support system and a key element of sustainable development. In turn the conservation of biodiversity requires sustainable land management.

Global biodiversity is being continuously eroded with thousands of species becoming extinct every year. We know very little about many of these species; they are not the 'headliners' such as blue whales or Siberian tigers. The UK has lost 100 species this century, mostly small insects. But however small, their place in the web of life is just as important.

Much of this loss is due to human activities. On a global scale, the destruction of the rainforest has been responsible for the extinction of many species, some of which we haven't known long enough to name. In the UK we cleared most of our forests years ago for agricultural, industrial and military purposes. We know that with those forests went many wild animals, such as bears and wolves, but what else did we lose? Whether or not we believe that each species has a moral right to exist, there is no doubt that their loss ultimately will be to the long-term detriment of humanity.

KEY LINKAGES:
*Other relevant sections of the guide are:
Built environment, Food*

Protecting biodiversity

At the United Nations Conference on Environment and Development in Rio de Janeiro 1992, 153 countries including the UK signed the Convention on Biological Diversity. Article 6a of the Convention requires each contracting party to: 'develop national strategies, plans or programmes for the conservation and sustainable use of biological diversity.'

To honour this obligation the UK government published *Biodiversity: the UK Action Plan* in 1994. Voluntary sector bodies including Butterfly Conservation, Friends of the Earth, Plantlife, RSPB, the Wildlife Trusts and WWF responded with their own 'Biodiversity Challenge'. Together these documents identify actions required at the national level to tackle the problems facing UK fauna and flora. The plans are based on the following principles:

- catalogue and describe the UK flora and fauna
- develop conservation priorities
- set realistic conservation targets
- quantify and understand the causes of changes in animal and plant abundance and distribution
- identify effective conservation actions
- monitor the success or failure of these actions.

The UK Biodiversity Action Group was set up to undertake the work outlined in the Action Plan. It has recommended costed action plans for conserving 116 species and 14 key habitats and issuing guidelines for the development of local biodiversity action plans (BAPs) as a means of implementing these plans. These guidelines have been produced in the form of a series of guidance notes published by the UK Biodiversity Group and the local government Improvement and Development Agency.

Local action

Many local biodiversity action plans have been developed, with different approaches and involving many different agencies. In most places local authorities are taking the lead but often by working through a local environmental forum, Local Agenda 21 group or some other community based group. For example, Mendip District Council (who produced one of the first local BAPs), used the skills of its own staff in partnership with Somerset Environmental Records Centre and English Nature. They identified action plans for habitats and species that were particularly threatened or distinctive of the local area. Species plans included the green-winged orchid, the marsh fritillary and the greater horseshoe bat.

Whilst the national action plan focuses mainly on rare species and endangered habitats, the local BAPs take a much broader approach. Small pockets of semi-natural greenspace are valued for their contribution to the conservation of the more common species as well as the rare. Without a network of more common species and habitats it becomes difficult for wildlife – common or rare – to move around the country and to maintain overall biodiversity. In urban areas, parks and gardens are key elements of conserving biodiversity, and brownfield sites often display a fascinating display of wild plants and animals.

Whatever the scale or the focus, the key points of a BAP are that the process and product are thoroughly researched, realistic in their approach and have involved the local community.

There are also other initiatives which are making a valuable contribution to conserving local biodiversity. For example, the organisation Common Ground helps people retain the crop biodiversity and local distinctiveness of their place by supporting a range of initiatives, including community orchards.

Thanks to these local and national initiatives the people of the UK can be assured that they will be making their contribution to conserving global biodiversity and ultimately the richness of human life.

Key organisations

Bat Conservation Trust
15 Cloisters House, 8 Battersea Park Road, London SW8 4BG Tel: 020 7627 2629 Fax: 020 7627 2628
Email: enquiries@bats.org.uk Website: www.bats.org.uk

The UK charity devoted to the conservation of bats. It runs the national Bat Helpline and the National Bat Monitoring Programme.

Butterfly Conservation
Conservation Office, PO Box 444, Wareham, Dorset BH20 5YA Tel: 01929 400209 Fax: 01929 400210
Email: ukconsoffice@butterfly-conservation.org

Butterfly Conservation is dedicated to securing a lasting future for all native butterflies and moths. It has drawn up action plans for threatened species and is leading work on butterfly and moth conservation in the UK.

Common Ground (see Main organisations)

Countryside Council for Wales
Head Office, Plas Penrhos, Ffordd Penrhos, Bangor, Gwynedd. LL57 2LQ Tel: 01248 385500
Website: www.ccw.gov.uk/

The Countryside Council for Wales is Government's statutory adviser on sustaining natural beauty, wildlife and opportunity for outdoor enjoyment in Wales and its inshore waters.

Department of the Environment, Transport and the Regions (DETR) Biodiversity Secretariat

Tollgate House, Houlton Street, Bristol, Avon BS2 9DJ Tel: 01179 878000 Fax: 01179 878182
Website: www.detr.gov.uk

Along with the Welsh Office and Scottish Office, DETR is responsible for supporting the UK Biodiversity Group. It publishes *Biodiversity News*.

English Nature

Northminster House, Peterborough PE1 1UA
Tel: 01733 455000 Fax: 01733 568834
Email: enquiries@english-nature.org.uk
Website: www.english-nature.org.uk/

English Nature is the official Government adviser on nature conservation in England and is responsible, both directly and through others, for the conservation of wildlife and natural features throughout England, including Sites of Special Scientific Interest and National Nature Reserves. Working in conjunction with its sister organisations, the Countryside Council for Wales and Scottish Natural Heritage, it produces a wealth of guidance and information on wildlife conservation.

Friends of the Earth (see Main organisations)

FoE has a long history of campaigning on site protection and is currently running a campaign on local wild places under threat.

IDA – Improvement and Development Agency (formerly Local Government Management Board)
(see Main organisations)

In conjunction with the UK Biodiversity Group, the IDA produced the series of Guidance Notes for local BAPs.

Landlife

National Wildflower Centre, Court Hey Park, Liverpool, L16 3NA Tel: 0151 737 1819 Fax: 0151 737 1820
Email: info@landlife.u-net.com
Website: www.merseysideworld.com/landlife

Landlife aims to increase wildflower resources for future generations by promoting the creation of new habitats that have economic, environmental, educational and ecological benefits for the nation. Since its establishment in 1975, Landlife has worked on a local and national level, with community participation always playing a key role.

Mendip District Council

Cannards Grave Road, Shepton Mallet, Somerset BA4 5BT Tel: 01749 343399 Fax: 01749 344050.

This small authority produced one of the first local BAPs.

Plantlife – The Wild Plant Conservation Charity

21 Elizabeth Street, London SW1W 9RP
Tel: 020 7808 0100 Fax: 020 7730 8377
Email: enquiries@plantlife.org.uk

Plantlife is active in campaigning for the conservation of plants at local, national and international levels.

Royal Society for the Protection of Birds

The Lodge, Sandy, Bedfordshire, SG19 2DL
Tel: 01767 680551 Website: www.rspb.org.uk

The RSPB works through a network of regional offices and is a key player in promoting BAPs.

Scottish Natural Heritage

12 Hope Terrace, Edinburgh EH9 2AS
Tel: 0131 447 4784 Fax: 0131 446 2277
Website: www.snh.org.uk/

Scottish Natural Heritage is Government's statutory adviser for wildlife in Scotland. Its aim is to help people enjoy Scotland's natural heritage responsibly, understand it more fully and use it wisely so that it can be sustained for future generations.

The Wildlife Trusts

The Royal Society for Nature Conservation (RSNC), The Kiln, Waterside, Mather Road, Newark NG24 1WT
Tel: 01636 670000 Fax: 01636 670001

RSNC is the national representative of all wildlife trusts throughout the UK. Each county in England and Wales, and several of the large urban areas including London and Birmingham, has a local wildlife trust active in conserving biodiversity. In Scotland it is the Scottish Wildlife Trust.

WWF UK (see Main organisations)

Further information

Publications

Biodiversity Action Plans – Case Studies and Guidance Notes. Examples of local BAPs, produced by the IDA and UK Biodiversity Group.

Making Biodiversity Happen – a supplementary consultation paper to *Opportunities for Change*. 1998. DETR, Eland House, Bressenden Place, London SW1E 5DU.

Actions for Biodiversity in the UK: approaches in UK to implementing the Convention on Biological Diversity. Hill, D., Treweek, J., Yates, T. & Pienkowski, M. (editors) 1996. Ecological Issues Series Publication No 6. British Ecological Society, London, UK.

Ideas into Action for Local Agenda 21. 1996. English Nature, Peterborough. ISBN 1 85716 208 0. £5.00.

Biodiversity Challenge – an agenda for conservation in the UK Wynne, G. et al. (second edition). 1995. RSPB, Sandy. ISBN 0 903138 80 8. £20.

UK Biodiversity Action Plan. CM2428. 1994. DETR, Eland House, Bressenden Place, London SW1E 5DU.

Sustainability in Practice. 1994. A report prepared for English Nature by David Tydesley and Associates, with CAG Consultants. English Nature, Peterborough. £12.50.

Energy use

'People do not need energy supply – they need the services energy gives them: warmth, light and equipment. Energy policy should be based on the principle of providing these energy services with less use of environmentally damaging forms of energy'

LGA position statement, 1998

Energy is essential to our lives, yet current practices of production, distribution and consumption cause many problems. Agenda 21 makes it clear that all energy use needs to respect the atmosphere, human health and the environment as a whole.

We all use energy all the time, whether by using transport, the washing machine or heating our homes. Most of the time we don't think about where it comes from. Nearly 80% of the energy we use is supplied through the burning of non-renewable fossil fuels. This releases carbon dioxide and other pollutants that contribute to the greenhouse effect, which in turn is producing global warming and climate change. While too much energy is wasted, many people in the UK also suffer from 'fuel poverty' – being short of money to pay for the energy they need in their daily lives.

Climate change – the biggest global problem

Climate change brought about by high levels of energy use is already becoming noticeable around the globe and is perhaps the most serious environmental threat we face. Carbon dioxide levels in the atmosphere are higher now at 358 parts per million by volume than at any time in human history. Governments and almost all scientists recognise the problem: the Kyoto Protocol, agreed in December 1997, set legally binding targets to reduce the emissions of greenhouse gases.

The United Kingdom has agreed to reduce its emissions to 12.5% below 1990 levels over the period 2008–2012. The Labour Government set a manifesto target of a 20% reduction in carbon dioxide emissions by 2010 and a 1999 commitment to 10% of the UK's electricity supplied from renewables by 2010 (just 2% in 1997).

Under the Home Energy Conservation Act, all local authorities have a duty to show the Secretary of State how they intend to reduce their output of CO_2 by 30%. Intentions are all well and good and some local authorities are taking their responsibility seriously but others have yet to put any initiatives into practice.

Affordable warmth

Most of us use far more energy than we need but almost a third of homes in Britain cannot afford enough energy to maintain a healthy comfortable living environment. Over eight million households suffer from fuel poverty. The Government has grouped these households into fuel poor, severe fuel poor and extreme fuel poor. Over one million households fall into the extreme fuel poor group. Extreme fuel poverty means that households need to spend up to 30% of their income on fuel to heat their homes adequately. Lone pensioners account for 44% of this group. In the winter of 1996–97, 46,000 more pensioners died than in the summer – a figure far higher than for Germany or Sweden, where winter temperatures are lower.

Poorer members of our society live in housing that is often much more expensive to heat than average, yet their incomes to meet this cost are lower. Caught between these two factors, they are forced to run up fuel debts or do without adequate levels of heating and lighting. Investigation has shown that those who live in poor housing visit the doctor more often and on average cost seven times as much in direct health costs as those who live in refurbished housing. It is estimated that poor energy inefficient housing costs the NHS £1 billion per annum.

Towards an energy efficient society

Moves towards sustainability mean we need to discourage excessive use of energy yet avoid discriminating against those who do not have affordable warmth. Energy efficiency cuts across all disciplines and boundaries and links health service providers, environmental health departments, social services, local environmental groups, economists and energy managers. For such disparate organisations to work together successfully is challenging, yet many lessons have already been learnt. Cross-departmental groups to stimulate local action are already in place in some areas. This work is being stimulated by Local Agenda 21 programmes that seek to set and implement targets for CO2 reduction by communities and councils working together.

National level action is likely to include 'carbon taxes' and further energy taxes, although there is concern that these may hit the poor hardest. Internationally it seems likely that 'carbon emission trading' will form part of the process to combat global warming. Meanwhile, large energy multi-nationals are already investing heavily in renewable energies and some forecasts suggest that 60–80% of the world's energy supply will come from these sources by 2100.

'Green energy' supplies

In September 1998 the Government introduced competition into the domestic energy market, which allows customers to choose which electricity company supplies their home. This opportunity to use purchasing power to favour power suppliers that provide 'green' energy (solar, water, wind, plant, energy efficiency and combined heat and power) could, over time, play a real role in the much-needed energy revolution.

A number of electricity suppliers have introduced 'green tariffs' for the domestic consumer. According to FoE, all green tariffs currently available involve payment of an additional premium. Generally speaking, two types are available: 'renewable tariffs', where for every unit of electricity used by a customer on a scheme, the supplier will buy a unit of electricity from a renewable source; and 'eco funds', where an additional customer premium is invested in new renewable energy products.

The Government's drive to promote *renewable energy* will also be crucial. Currently the UK is focusing on energy efficiency measures to meet its climate change obligations. This has resulted in other renewable energy technologies such as solar power being under-developed in the UK, resulting in higher manufacturing and system costs. Despite that, many people are investing in renewables, and expert advice is widely available.

Solar clubs are an excellent example of how energy efficiency advice centres, local authorities and community groups can work to increase the use of solar energy technology in their area. Solar clubs are about making solar water heating more cost effective and accessible. They enable interested householders to join together in order to install equipment, share tools and labour, have access to professional technical support and pool purchasing power to buy equipment at bulk discounts.

If real progress is to be made there must be a concerted effort to connect people with the policy processes. There is much that individuals and communities can do to reduce the energy we use but as yet, relatively few people understand the immense environmental and social challenges that global warming brings. If we are to meet these challenges, an enormous educational process is needed. Government, industry and the voluntary sector will need to work together to ensure that solutions are just and equitable.

Key organisations

Each of the groups listed here can either help directly or will advise on the most appropriate group to consult.

Age Concern
Astral House, 1268 London Road, London SW16 4ER
Tel: 020 8679 8000 Fax: 020 8679 6069
Website: www.ace.org.uk

Age Concern undertakes research into fuel poverty and runs initiatives such as Safe and Warm, a home-visiting energy-advice service and similar outreach work.

Association for the Conservation of Energy (ACE)
Westgate House, Prebend Street, London N1 8PT
Tel: 080 7359 8000 Fax: 080 7389 0863
Email: aceuk@aol.com
Website: www.members.aol.com/aceuk/home.htm

ACE is a lobbying group carrying out policy research on energy conservation. Members include companies that have interests in energy conservation equipment and services. An information pack is available.

Carbon Storage Trust
11 King Edward Street, Oxford OX1 4HT
Tel: 01865 244151 Fax: 01865 243499
Email: mail@co2.org Website: www.co2.org

This is an independent company which operates the Climate Care label scheme for all types of products that do not add to global warming, with a focus on energy efficiency, renewables and reforestation.

Centre for Alternative Technology (CAT)
(see Main organisations)

Energy Conservation & Solar Centre (ECSC)
Unit 325/6, 30 Great Guildford Street, London SE1 0HS
Tel: 020 7207 9052 Fax: 020 7207 8880
Email: energy.ecsc@dial.pipex.com

ECSC is an educational charity active in community level energy initiatives. It trains local voluntary networks to deliver energy advice and stimulate improvements and runs an advice service for low income households. ECSC has a resource pack, *Energy Resources for Tenants*, and is preparing a solar energy directory. It has a telephone support service for Local Agenda 21 officers and runs the Tenants Energy Advice Service in Greater London.

Energy Efficiency Advice Centres

There are about 40 local centres around the UK that comprise the National Energy Efficiency Advice Centre Network (often referred to as EEACs). The centres provide simple, free energy surveys that the householder completes and returns by freepost to their local centre. They are processed and the enquirer is sent a printed report that itemises possible energy improvements and the likely savings. Although originally intended for owner-occupier households, many of the centres also operate other local projects on energy and can give advice on local contacts and grant assistance.

To contact your nearest centre, use the national freephone number 0800 512012.

Energy Efficiency Best Practice Programme

A government initiative managed jointly by BRECSU, for buildings, and ETSU, for industry, on behalf of DETR. Energy and Environment helpline – Tel: 0800 585 794

Energy Saving Trust
21 Dartmouth Street, London SW1 HPB
Tel: 020 7931 8401 Fax: 020 7654 2444
Website: www.est.org.uk
Energy efficiency telephone helpline on 0345 277 200

This Government-funded trust promotes the efficient use of energy by sponsoring energy saving initiatives such as the Energy Efficiency Advice Centres and promoting initiatives that reduce greenhouse gas emissions. Many of their schemes for domestic homes concentrate on promotions and offers, usually provided by a discount or a cashback towards the cost of buying energy efficient goods and services. Schemes promoted through the Trust vary so check with your local EEAC for up to date advice. (They can be contacted on 0800 512 012.) It also produces a wide range of free leaflets on domestic energy efficiency.

Friends of the Earth (see Main organisations)
Published a *Guide to Buying Green Energy, September 1998.* This short consumer guide provides the information necessary to select the greenest energy supplier.

Local councils
Local authorities have a duty to reduce fuel consumption in their housing stock. This includes both public and private sector homes. Your local council will have appointed a specific officer to oversee this work, usually referred to as the HECA Officer. This officer may be based in a number of different departments so can be difficult to track down. If you have problems finding the appropriate officer, contact the Energy Conservation & Solar Centre (see above), who may be able to help you.

Local Government Association (LGA)
(see Main organisations)

Has issued a position statement on energy services for sustainable communities (1998). This is the most comprehensive argument yet for pursuing sustainable energy strategies at the local and national level. It asks for the powers and resources to enable local government to play a full part in providing the solutions for more sustainable local communities. A full report is also available.

Neighbourhood Energy Action (NEA)
St Andrews House, 90-92 Pilgrim Street,
Newcastle upon Tyne NE1 6SG Tel: 0191 261 5677
Fax: 0191 261 6496 Email: nea@nea.org.uk
Website: www.nea.org.uk

NEA is a well-established national organisation providing training and advice on fuel poverty. It operates a number of local projects, produces a members' newsletter and a range of other publications on energy efficiency and affordable warmth issues.

Office of Electricity Regulation (Offer)
Exists to protect the interests of all electricity consumers. A free information booklet on customer choice in electricity supply is available from Freephone 0800 451 451 or from Hagley House, 83–85 Hagley Road, Edgbaston, Birmingham B16 8QG Tel: 0121 456 2100

Solar Century
5 Sandycombe Centre, Sandycombe Road,
Richmond TW9 2EP Fax: 0870 7358101
Email: webmaster@solarcentury.co.uk

A group campaigning for green energy, seeking to develop a network of 'show homes' that will produce more electricity than they consume.

Wind and Sun Ltd
Humber Marsh, Stoke Prior, Leominster,
Herefordshire HR6 0NE Tel: 01568 760671
Fax: 01568 760484 Website: www.windandsun.co.uk

Wind and Sun has been using, living with and installing wind and solar power since 1984, so advice and product selection is based on 'hands-on' experience. It has a workshop, showroom, test and demonstration site where many items can be seen on working display (by appointment). A design guide and catalogue is available price £5 + £1 p&p and an increasing amount of information is available electronically.

Further information

Publications and videos

Green Energy: Local Agenda 21 in action – 30 minute video reviews some real-life sustainable energy projects around the UK and demonstrates how they relate to LA21 initiatives. Contact NATTA, c/o EERU, Open University, Milton Keynes MK7 6AA.

Energy Saving Guide for Small Businesses. BRESCU/BRE for DETR. July 1997.

The National Solar Clubs Manual. Centre for Sustainable Energy and Environ. 1998

Domestic and Commercial Solar Energy in the UK – Research Report. Energy Conservation and Solar Centre 1999. £25. This report demonstrates the potential for solar power in the UK and argues that although the technology has existed for some time and systems are considered robust and reliable, it is still perceived by many as 'cutting edge'. It calls for Government to support a package of suggested measures but highlights that other stakeholders (industry, business and local authorities) must also make a move in the solar direction.

Websites

www.energy21.org.uk – This website focuses on the use of renewable energy in the local environment.

Sustainable waste management and recycling

'Environmentally sound waste management must go beyond the mere safe disposal or recovery of wastes that are generated and seek to address the root cause of the problem by attempting to change unsustainable patterns of production and consumption'.

Chapter 21, Agenda 21

Waste is an inevitable byproduct of human activity so there is an urgent need to develop sustainable waste management strategies. Agenda 21 warns that without remedial action, world production of solid waste could increase by four or five times by 2025. In addition to solid wastes (domestic refuse, non-hazardous wastes such as commercial and institutional wastes, street sweepings and construction debris) there are rising quantities of sewage, hazardous materials and radioactive wastes presenting threats to humanity and biodiversity.

Reducing our use of resources and energy is a central plank of developing a sustainable economy. This can improve social equity – at present 20% of the world's population consumes 80% of the resources – while waste management creates jobs and helps with economic development. The UK generates 27 million tonnes of domestic waste a year (approximately 1 tonne per household), so there is plenty of scope for change. While individual action is important, sustainable waste management requires strategic leadership from Government, backed by incentives and economic instruments to encourage the necessary changes.

Agenda 21 identified four specific areas for action:

- increasing waste minimisation
- maximising environmentally sound re-use and recycling
- setting international standards for waste treatment and disposal
- extending waste services by ensuring frameworks and infrastructures are in place.

KEY LINKAGES:
*Other relevant sections of this Guide are:
Business; Built environment; Sustainable livelihoods;
Consumption, Energy*

Finding the best way forward

The Government White Paper 'Making Waste Work' (1995) was the UK's first attempt to define a national waste strategy within a context of sustainable development. Its key objectives were:

- to reduce the amount of waste produced
- to make the best use of what waste is produced
- to choose waste management practices that minimise the risks of immediate and future environmental pollution and harm to human health.

Revised key goals are:

- to recycle or compost 30% of household waste by 2010
- to recover 45% of municipal waste by 2010.

A revised national strategy will be published late 1999. The consultation draft, 'A Way with Waste', called for enhanced waste minimisation and recycling as a priority; in some sectors the amount of waste generated is growing by 3% a year. It also called for substantial investment in incineration. The new waste strategy is expected to develop the existing policy of implementing the waste hierarchy and the 'Best Practicable Environmental Option'. This entails finding the best practicable means for dealing with a particular process or substance to remove or reduce its impact on the environment.

Making it happen

All sectors agree that more action is needed: the potential is 'currently obstructed by collection, regulation, and management regimes mitigating against economies of scale.' (Biffa Waste Services). Only 8% of household waste is recycled and a further 6% has energy recovered from it so the 25% recycling target (by 2005, and 30% by 2010) is a daunting one. There is however considerable variation in the performance of local authorities: some have already topped the 25% target. Most local authorities now have recycling officers to act as a focal point for recycling initiatives. The Government's Select Committee (1998) noted that 'local government must also play a part by the operation of green procurement policies' to help stimulate demand for recycled content products and materials. The new Best Value regime for procurement of local authority services should help.

Forward-looking waste management companies increasingly view themselves as resource managers and are incorporating the broader sustainability agenda into their operations. The landfill tax, due to rise to £15 per tonne by 2004, is the Government's main instrument for encouraging change in the commercial sector. The Environmental Technology Best Practice Programme is also promoting good practice and waste minimisation, and there are now about 50 business waste minimisation clubs throughout the UK.

Nationally, measures such as the UK Landfill Tax, Producer Responsibility Obligations on packaging and the forthcoming EU Landfill Directive will add to the costs of waste disposal, making waste minimisation, re-use, and recycling in all sectors increasingly attractive. Currently there are various 'market failures' which give primary materials an unfair advantage over recovered or recycled (secondary) materials. These include:

- the failure to include environmental 'externalities' in the prices of primary and secondary materials
- the absence of standards for recycled materials
- public perceptions that recycled products are inferior and more expensive
- the small number of reprocessors for some materials.

Waste reduction

Minimising waste by changing lifestyles and consumption patterns offers the best chance for reversing current trends. Waste reduction targets should influence patterns of production and consumption, while more research is needed on clean technologies, along with incentives for reducing waste. Reducing the distance waste has to travel for disposal is of great importance to sustainability considerations.

To many people waste minimisation means recycling, although reuse and reduction should be higher priorities. The UK's largest waste awareness campaign, targeting the general public, will be launched early in 2000. It is supported by a broad spectrum of organisations, including Government, and will link into the UK's strategy for sustainable development and the DETR's 'Are You Doing Your Bit' campaign. Its broad objectives are:

- to move waste up the environmental agenda
- to increase the level of awareness as to why people should think and act differently about waste
- to increase the level of individual responsibility for waste
- to overcome current inertia and make action to reduce, reuse, and recycle an imperative.

Reuse it!

Much of what is thrown away as waste can be reused. Around the world there are plenty of examples of industry, public sector and voluntary groups working together to reuse materials and to get them back into the cycles of production rather than going to landfill or incineration. In the UK there are many employment training projects for people facing disadvantage that have clear environmental and social benefits. Community-based projects are taking unwanted furniture, white goods (fridges and cookers), computers and electrical items and restoring and refurbishing them for resale or donation to those in need.

Other sectors identified for action include the construction and demolition industry. The UK used 208 million tonnes of primary aggregates in 1996, but reused or recycled only 13.5 million tonnes of the 30 million tonnes of waste it produced. Sustainable construction initiatives and waste exchange networks are now run by many groups, including the Building Research Establishment (BRE).

Recycling

Maximising environmentally sound waste reuse and recycling is an option that will become more economically attractive as disposal sites are filled or closed and might require economic, market and legal incentives.

Close the loop!

Developing a recycling infrastructure that supports new jobs and products can be a win-win situation for everyone, and increasing the markets for recycled products must be a key part of that development. Some specific policy measures and incentives are now needed to encourage manufacturers to use recycled materials and large organisations to buy products made from those recycled materials. To get to a point where everyone can 'buy recycled' there needs to be a long-term programme including:

- development of national policies and regulation
- setting of performance standards of materials
- better procurement practices
- information and education programmes.

Take it back!

In the long term 'Producer Responsibility' is the key: those who create waste should share responsibility for it. This should influence the design of products to avoid waste in their manufacture and use, and to ensure environmentally responsible disposal at the end of their lifecycle. In its 1998 report, the House of Commons Environment Committee viewed producer responsibility as an 'exciting concept' with significant potential to encourage more sustainable patterns of resource use.

At present, legislation has only been introduced for commercial packaging but discussions are under way within the European Commission to extend the concept to cover end-of-life vehicles, batteries, electric and electronic goods. This could lead to 'product takeback', where manufacturers would be obliged to take back obsolete goods, such as out-dated computers, and re-use parts or dispose of them safely.

Cutting down on landfill

The Landfill Tax is the UK's first 'green tax'. It is still low at just £10 a tonne for active waste from April 1999. Inert waste is taxed at £2 per tonne although since October 1999, if this waste is used for landfill restoration it is tax exempt.

Despite the low cost of landfill, the tax has started making companies rethink their handling and disposal methods with an emphasis on reduction, reuse and recycling. The tax also helps the environment. Since 1996, landfill operators have diverted £135 million of landfill tax credits to environmental bodies in the UK carrying out environmental improvement and sustainable waste management research and education projects. The DETR is considering how the scheme might be changed to encourage more recycling. There are now calls for a tax on incineration, similar to the landfill tax, in order to 'level the playing field'.

Key organisations

The waste industry includes private companies, trade associations, professional institutes, local government organisations and not-for-profit groups, each with their own strengths in terms of information provision, promotion and education campaigns.

Building Research Establishment (BRE)
(see Main organisations)

BREs cover waste as part of the work on the built environment. Website: www.helios.bre.co.uk/waste/

Community Composting Network (CCN)
67 Alexandra Rd. Sheffield, S Yorks S2 3EE
Tel/Fax: 0114 258 0483 Email: heeleyfarm@gn.apc.org
Website: www.chiron-s.demon.co.uk/ccn/

CCN provides advice and support to composting projects across the UK.

Community Recycling Network (CRN)
10-12 Picton Street, Montpelier, Bristol BS6 5QA
Tel: 0117 942 0142 Fax: 0117 942 0164
Email: crnmail@crnhq.demon.co.uk
Website: crnhq.demon.co.uk/

CRN is an umbrella body for about 200 community-based waste projects and businesses. Collectively these employ about 500 people, offer places to 3,000 volunteers and provide recycling services to an estimated 4.5 million people in the UK.

Computer Recycling
Recycle-IT! c/o SKF (UK), Sundon Park Road, Luton LU3 3 BL Tel: 01582 492436 Fax: 01582 597778
Email: recycle_it@cix.co.uk

Recycle-IT! is one of many projects around the UK that takes ageing computers and refurbishes them for use by communities in the UK or abroad.

Furniture Recycling Network
c/o SOFA, Unit 3 Pilot House, King Street, Leicester LE1 6RN Tel: 0116 254 5283 Fax: 0116 254 4189
Email: frn@btinternet.com

Can provide extensive advice on setting up a community-based furniture recycling project.

Friends of the Earth (FoE) (see Main organisations)

Henry Doubleday Research Association
(see Main organisations)

Save Waste and Prosper (SWAP)
74 Kirkgate, Leeds, West Yorkshire LS2 7DJ
Tel: 0113 243 8777 Fax: 0113 234 4222
Email: swap@geo2.poptel.org.uk

Specialises in sustainable resource management, waste minimisation and recycling. Joint co-ordinators of the new National Waste Awareness Initiative.

Waste Watch
Europa House, Ground Floor, 13-17 Ironmonger Row, London EC1V 3QN Tel: 020 7253 6266
Fax: 020 7253 5962 Website: www.wastewatch.org.uk

A leading, cross-sectoral national organisation that educates, informs, and raises awareness on waste reduction, re-use and recycling. A charity, it provides information, consultancy, training events and campaigning and advocacy for all sectors and manages the National Recycling Forum with whom it jointly published the 'UK Recycled Products Guide' 1999 and developed the associated Buy Recycled web site.

Wastebusters Ltd
3rd Floor, Brighton House, Brighton Terrace, London SW9 8DJ
Tel: 020 7207 3434 Fax: 020 7207 2051

Small consultancy aiming to develop sound environmental practice in offices, by providing practical assistance. Co-ordinates the Waste Alert network of business waste minimisation groups in London.

Women's Environmental Network (WEN)
1st Floor, Worship Street, London EC2A 2BE
Tel: 020 7247 3327 Fax: 020 7247 4740
Email: wenuk@gn.apc.org
Website: www.gn.apc.org/wen

Particularly strong on waste reduction and re-use initiatives at the individual and community level.

World Resource Foundation
Heath House, 133 High Street, Tonbridge, Kent TN9 1DH Tel: 01732 368333 Fax: 01732 368337
Email: wrf@wrf.org.uk Website: www.wrf.org.uk

Provides an information service on the sustainable management of, and recovery of resources from, post-consumer wastes. Publishes the WARMER Bulletin six times a year (subscription basis) and has an excellent web site.

Further information

Publications

Less Waste, More Value – consultation paper (DETR 1998) and draft strategy – *'A Way with Waste'* (June 1999) on future waste options. Available on DETR website www.detr.gov.uk or through DETR free literature service.

Policy Instruments to Correct Market Failure in the Demand for Secondary Materials (Ecotec) 1999 (99EP0360) available from DETR Free Literature Service.

Shared Advantage: allies in waste prevention WEN 1999. £2.50 or free on website.

Websites

Aluminium Can Recycling Association: www.alucan.org.uk

British Glass: www.britglas.co.uk

British Plastics Federation: www.bpf.co.uk

Buy Recycled Web Site – National Recycling Forum/Waste Watch: www.nrf.org.uk

Centre for Sustainable Design: www.cfsd.org.uk

Entrust: www.entrust.org.uk

Environmental Bodies' Council (ebco): www.ebco.org.uk

Industry Council for Packaging and the Environment: www.incpen.org

SALVO (architectural salvage & reclaimed materials): www.salvo.co.uk

Steel Can Recycling Information Bureau: www.scrib.org

Telephone helplines

Environmental helpline – 0800 585794
Email: etbppenvhelp@aeat.co.uk
Website: www.etsu.com/etbpp/

Waste Watch's Wasteline – 0870 2430136. A free telephone information service providing guidance on materials reuse and recycling, products made from recycled materials, community projects, local authority recycling services and facilities, and contacts for environmental organisations and trade associations. Also see information and policy material on www.wastewatch.org.uk

● Water

'Safe water supplies and environmental sanitation are vital for protecting the environment, improving health and alleviating poverty.'

Chapter 18, Agenda 21

'The management and use of water resources must contribute towards sustainable development whilst protecting the aquatic environment and facilitating economic growth and higher living standards.'

UK Government's response to ACBE report,
October 1998

Availability of fresh water remains one of the limiting factors for sustainable development. Globally, 1.3 billion people lack access to an adequate supply of safe water and 25 million people die each year from diseases caused by unsafe drinking water and a lack of water for sanitation and hygiene. Over half these deaths are young children. 1 in 7 people in Europe lack access to safe drinking water – in developing countries it is 1 in 4.

Here in the UK a constant supply of clean water is taken for granted. The entire supply system is treated to a potable (drinking) standard even though just 3% is used for cooking and drinking. Achieving a balance between supply and demand is crucial for future sustainability. Water is abstracted from rivers, reservoirs and lakes (surface water) and from groundwater supplies held underground in porous rock aquifers. Increasing urbanisation and the unpredictability of climate change creates uncertainties in terms of future water demand. Water efficiency and conservation measures are therefore vital. The DETR has called for management which meets society's 'need for water in a fair and affordable way.'

The water industry (including sewerage) was privatised in 1989. Over the last decade prices have risen sharply – three times the rate of inflation – partly as a result of increased expenditure by companies to meet European regulations on water quality. The Director General of OFWAT, the industry regulator, announced price limits in July 1999 to cut water bills by an average of £38 by 2004–5. A wholesale review of the industry is scheduled; from the year 2004, the Secretary of State will have the option of giving a company a 10 year notice. Revocation of an operational licence is thus perceived as a permanent and credible threat. Commentators note that this provides a powerful opportunity for rethinking more sustainable management of the water industry.

In October 1998 guidance issued by the DETR demanded cleaner water at lower cost. Proposals included:

- calls for an end to all 'significant discharges' of untreated or so-called primary treated sewage
- a ban on use of untreated sludge on agricultural land after 2001
- compliance with EU Bathing Water Directive
- substantial investment to replace pipework by 2010, to control Cryptosporidium, and to meet mandatory obligations under the new EC Drinking Water Directive, including lead reductions, largely by 2003
- more infrastructure investment.

KEY LINKAGES:
Other relevant sections of this Guide are: Health, Biodiversity

Water quality and health

There is much debate over the quality of drinking water despite improvements in recent years. Measures to comply with European regulations are behind schedule. There is growing concern about the extent of contamination of vital underground water reserves, which supply over 35% of our drinking water. Threats to water quality include contamination by chemicals, pollution from organic materials and over-abstraction of supplies to meet rising demand. Traditional methods of industrial waste-water disposal such as dilution and dispersion into rivers are increasingly questioned as growing evidence of environmental damage emerges. The long-term health impact of 'cocktails' of pesticides, fertilisers and other chemicals is unknown but evidence already shows deleterious effects on human health and damage to ecological systems.

Lead remains an area of concern. It is estimated that 45% of households in Britain use water that, at some stage, has passed through lead piping. Such pipes were banned in new buildings back in 1976 but a problem remains with lead solder in copper piping and connections. Lead is a powerful neuro-toxin with no safe level of exposure. It has been linked with reduced intelligence in children and it is toxic to the unborn child.

Research published by the Drinking Water Inspectorate (1998) revealed that only 7 out of 10 people are satisfied with their drinking water quality – the main complaints being taste, cloudiness and discoloration.

Sewage disposal, water quality and beaches

The UK generates more than 30 million tonnes of sewage sludge each year – in the past 25% was dumped at sea. In January 1999 the EU Urban Wastewater Treatment Directive came into force banning dumping of sewage in coastal waters. Alternative disposal routes include: spreading on agricultural land – although this has raised food safety concerns if left untreated; disposal to landfill or incineration – both costly and the latter does not utilise the nutrient content. Proposals now include sludge drying to produce soil conditioners and fertilisers.

Significant health risks are posed by the pathogenic viruses and bacteria contained in sewage. Surfers Against Sewage (SAS) are calling for all sewage to be fully treated before disposal, and for both the liquid and solid waste to be treated as a resource rather than a waste. Full treatment cuts health risks and SAS claim that the cost is equal to or cheaper than the 'pump and dump' mentality of long sea outfall pipes.

Litter and other discarded materials on beaches remain a problem leading to undesirable environmental impacts and loss of amenity value.

Everybody lives downstream ...

Indiscriminate dumping occurs every day; impacts range from the deliberate release of toxic materials into watercourses through to incidents arising from a lack of awareness. For example, one litre of waste oil can pollute up to one million litres of water. The percentage of waste oil recovered from DIY motorists is much lower than that recovered from industry – less than 50%.

Water conservation and efficiency measures

Every sector could use water more efficiently and reduce overall consumption. At the 1997 Water Summit, the Government asked all water companies to prepare drought contigency and water resource plans looking 25 years ahead. It is expected that the Government will make such plans a statutory requirement. The promotion of water re-use activities by industry, irrespective of whether drought conditions exist, is encouraged wherever practicable. Mandatory leakage targets are now in place.

New regulations to protect water quality and supplies came into effect on 1 July 1999. They include restrictions on the flush volume on new WCs to 6 litres and on the water consumption of some other household appliances such as washing machines and dishwashers. Opinions differ on whether water meters (pay for what you use) cut usage; Anglian Water reports that customers who have adopted water meters have cut usage by 23% whilst others argue that the costs just tend to get absorbed within household expenditure.

Active consideration is being given to issues such as making greater use of grey-water (run-off from buildings, 'clean' water from rain run-off, baths, showers, sinks etc). Many efficiency techniques are already being incorporated into the design and planning stage of buildings e.g. low flush toilets and urinals. Information on such activities is available from statutory authorities and others such as the National Water Demand Management Centre. Experimental schemes adopting clean technologies such as use of reed beds for sewage purification (e.g. Wessex Water) are underway in many locations.

Water use at the household level

At the household level, water companies, often acting in partnership with local authorities, are promoting special offers on water butts for rainwater collection and most water companies offer water 'hippos' – plastic devices put in toilet cisterns – to reduce water use per flush. Other options include simple measures like mending dripping taps, through to use of low-water irrigation systems for the garden and planting drought-resistant plants in both the household and municipal situation.

Key organisations

Centre for Alternative Technology (CAT)
(see Main organisations)

DETR (see Main organisations)
Draft water regulations are available from DETR Free literature

Environment Agency
General enquiry line 0645 333111.
Emergency 24 hour hotline for reporting all pollution incidents 0800 807060.

Environment and Energy Helpline
0800 585794
Promotes better environmental practices that reduce business costs for UK industry.

Friends of the Earth (see Main organisations)

Marine Conservation Society
9 Gloucester Road, Ross-on-Wye, Herefordshire HR9 5BU Tel: 01989 566 Email: mcsuk@mcmail.com
Website: www.mcsuk.mcmail.com

The MCS campaigns on issues that affect the sea and seashore.

National Water Demand Management Centre
Environment Agency, Guildborne House, Chatsworth Road, Worthing, West Sussex BN11 1LD
Tel: 01903 832275 Fax: 01903 832274
Email: wdmc@ dial.pipex.com

Surfers Against Sewage (SAS)
2 Rural Workshops, Wheal Kitty, St Agnes, Cornwall TR5 0RD Tel: 01872 553001 Fax: 01872 552615
Email: info@ sas.org.uk Website: www.sas.org.uk

A nationwide campaign for clean seas, and not just for surfers. SAS runs high profile, media-oriented legal and political campaigns opposed to the dumping of sewage and toxic materials at sea. It organises and supports scientific research and has acted as an independent adviser to Government. Issues a quarterly newsletter.

WaterAid
Tel: 020 7793 4500

A charity set up in 1981 by UK water companies in response to UN's Decade of Drinking Water and Sanitation. It works through partner organisations in developing countries to encourage self-help and access to improved water supplies.

Water UK
1 Queen Anne's Gate, London SW1H 9BT
Tel: 020 7344 1844 Fax: 020 7957 4666

This trade association for the water industry published an initial set of 25 indicators in 1999 designed to 'track the year-on-year progress of sustainability throughout the industry'. They include: provision of water services; environmental management; local environment and biodiversity; energy and material flows.

Further information

Publications

Saving Water – on the right track. National Centre for Water Demand Management. January 1998. Short profiles and case studies ranging from rain water harvesting and low water gardens to water metering, business waste minimisation schemes and water management in buildings.

Websites

www.databases.detr.gov.uk/water/index.htm – A new internet database aimed at helping the water industry, plumbers, architects and environmental organisations to 'do their bit' to conserve water. The database holds details of over 200 research projects and case studies investigating all aspects of water conservation, and is a joint initiative between DETR and Environment Agency's National Water Demand Management Centre.

3 Getting around

● Integrated and sustainable transport

THERE IS LITTLE MENTION OF TRANSPORT IN AGENDA 21, yet it has become very clear in the UK that transport issues are at the heart of sustainable development. The most obvious issues are the environmental ones: air pollution, land use, etc. but there are also huge social implications. Cost-effective, more efficient, less polluting, safer rural and urban mass transit should be developed and promoted, and national transport and settlement planning integrated.

Transport does not always get the notice it deserves in health promotion and anti-poverty strategies, but recent developments and consumer pressure are pushing transport higher up these agendas. After years of neglect, there are new pressures in favour of an increase in the quality, quantity and accessibility of public transport, and for more resources to be directed towards the 'slow' modes of travel: walking and cycling.

KEY LINKAGES:
*Other relevant sections of this guide are:
Built environment, Health, Energy*

Current issues in the UK

The car now influences every aspect of people's lives, creating car dependency. This has led to a lack of investment in the other modes of travel, making the alternatives to the car appear unattractive. A sustainable transport system will require not just new investment, but also cultural change – an enormous challenge.

Integrated transport

This new mood was captured in the Government's White Paper (July 1998) on the future of transport, *A New Deal for Transport: Better for Everyone*. This was the first national statement of transport strategy and policies for 20 years. It outlined the Government's commitment to developing and implementing an integrated transport strategy.

Implementation and the associated costs are now causing problems, alongside a widespread perception that rail services are declining in quality and reliability, something that puts people off leaving their cars at home. For councils, the Government White Paper (and its 'daughter' document on tackling traffic congestion, *Breaking The Logjam*) holds out the prospect of charging people for using their cars on certain road networks, and for workplace parking.

Green transport plans

Hospitals and other health facilities within the National Health Service experience major problems due to over-dependence on the car by staff, patients and visitors. Many other large employers face the same issues. The response is to develop 'green transport plans'. All major Government offices were instructed to have a plan in place by 31 March 1999. In June 1999 the DETR produced a guidebook: *Preparing your organisation for transport in the future: the benefits of Green Transport Plans*. This is designed for managers in business and other organisations: it explains how such plans can improve access for staff and customers, cut congestion and parking costs, and help run car fleets more efficiently.

Congestion is costing commerce and business millions of pounds. There is support from many major businesses and employers' organisations for commuter travel planning, which will necessitate higher investment in public transport, walking and cycling. Gradually, local green transport co-ordinators and mobility advisors are being employed by businesses, councils and central government to promote green transport plans.

Travel to school

Car journeys to school have grown rapidly over the last ten years, adding to congestion during the morning rush hour. The need to tackle this issue and encourage more walking, cycling and bus travel to schools is a priority. The Government, Transport 2000, and the Walk-to-School campaign have all produced material on this topic.

Road danger reduction

Councils are responsible for overseeing road danger reduction, and new road safety targets are being established. Motor vehicle occupants are experiencing fewer fatal and serious injuries in road traffic accidents, but the threat to pedestrians – especially children – is still very serious.

Social inclusion

Renewed interest from the Government in social exclusion highlights the need for interventions to prevent it, for increased co-ordination of effort, and for innovation. All these measures will require affordable, accessible and reliable alternatives to the car in order for everyone to get to and from work or training.

Independent living

Public transport needs to be accessible for disabled people. Lack of mobility presents disabled people with a perennial obstacle to independent living, and leads to poor health and fewer educational, employment and social opportunities. The Disability Discrimination Act (DDA) is creating minimum technical specifications for accessible taxis, buses and trains, which operators must meet. But the DDA does not provide a right in law to ride public transport. The Government has said it will introduce civil rights for disabled people that are comprehensive and enforceable.

Direct payments to disabled people, in place of traditional forms of provision by health and social services departments, are now possible. This will increase the demand for more accessible taxis and other door-to-door services.

Local air quality and health

Councils have new responsibilities for local air quality management and are under pressure to tackle poor air quality. In urban areas, much of this is caused by road traffic. In response, councils are expected to improve the alternatives to the private car. The Road Traffic Reduction Act 1997 provides local government with new powers to set targets for limiting traffic growth. Government discussions on public health have explicitly linked poor health, in its broadest sense, with community isolation and lack of access to amenities. Community isolation has often been caused by road building, and out-of-town retail, leisure and health facilities are often out of reach to people with no access to a car.

'Active for Life'

There are many health promotion campaigns in favour of regular physical exercise, including Health at Work groups. Implicitly, these campaigns seek less use of the car and therefore underpin the demand for better walking and cycling provision, and improved public transport.

The international perspective

All these pressures point towards the adoption of transport policies which promote sustainable development. The summits held at Rio and Kyoto have made a direct impact on how councils in particular approach transport policy development. Most Local Agenda 21 initiatives contain specific transport-related actions designed to reduce CO_2 emissions. The European Commission is also devoting a significant amount of its research and development budget to sustainable transport initiatives. In 1999 the World Health Organisation launched its European Charter on Transport, Health and the Environment, the first international agreement on these issues. It is now hoped that this Charter will develop into a legally binding Convention, setting common standards for Europe.

Local action

While a new political approach and better infrastructure are vital, individuals can help make change. Many small-scale actions can combine to make a major impact. Individuals can make fewer car-based journeys each week, occasionally work from home, make it practical for their child to walk or cycle to school, use Internet home shopping services, and generally undertake fewer journeys. A school can encourage safe routes to school, and make better use of shared transport solutions (minibus, coach, train). A company can adopt a staff travel policy which removes transport from the remuneration package, encourages sustainable travel options, and reduces the overall need to travel on business.

Key organisations

There are many integrated and sustainable transport initiatives, research projects, and experiments taking place in the UK. These are just a few but form useful starting points.

Association for Commuter Transport (ACT)
c/o PTRC ERS Limited, Glenthorne House,
Hammersmith Grove, London W6 0LG
Tel: 020 8741 1516 Fax: 020 8741 5993
Email: mail@ptrcers.demon.co.uk

ACT is a new organisation, which produces a newsletter and factsheets and has held 'master-classes' and seminars. It is seeking to attract private sector company members.

Community Car Share Network (CCSN)
The Studio, 32 The Calls, Leeds LS2 7EW
Tel: 0113 234 9299 Fax: 0113 242 3687
Email: office@carshareclubs.org.uk
Website: www.carshareclubs.org.uk

CCSN helps develop city car clubs and their rural counterparts. It runs an information service and website, and through its RideSmart programme, provides development support to car-sharing projects in England.

Cyclists' Touring Club (CTC)
69 Meadrow, Godalming, Surrey GU7 3HS
Tel: 01483 417217 Fax: 01483 426994
Email: cycling@ctc.org.uk

CTC is the major lobbying organisation for cyclists, and produces a lot of information and advice materials. It organises National Bike Week each June, with thousands of local events.

Don't Choke Britain
c/o NEXUS, Cuthbert House, All Saints,
Newcastle upon Tyne NE1 2DA Tel: 0191 203 3233
Fax: 0191 203 3180 Website: www.dcb.org.uk

Don't Choke Britain is a collaborative campaign run every June, led by the Local Government Association and the national Passenger Transport Executive Group, and now involving over 30 national partner organisations including the Health Education Authority and the Government. It supports local initiatives that aim to encourage motorists to take the first steps towards changing their habits. It supports Green Transport Week and National Car-Free Day, National Bike Week and Walk to School initiatives and provides free leaflets, posters and advice packs.

Environmental Transport Association (ETA)
10 Church Street, Weybridge, Surrey KT13 8RS
Tel: 0193 282 8882 Fax: 0193 282 9015
Website: www.eta.co.uk

The ETA promotes Green Transport Week and National Car-Free Day, and offers a driver support scheme similar to that run by the AA and RAC.

Friends of the Earth (see Main organisations)

Pedestrians Association (PA)
31-33 Bondway, London SW8 1SJ Tel: 020 7820 1010
Fax: 020 7820 8208 Email: info@pedestrians.org.uk
Website: www.pedestrians.org.uk

The PA campaigns for a better deal for pedestrians. It also runs the Walk to School Campaign.

Sustrans
35 King Street, Bristol BS1 4DZ Tel: 0117 926 8893
Fax: 0117 929 4173 Website: www.sustrans.org.uk

Sustrans has been developing the national cycling network and work on safe routes to school promotion.

Transport 2000 (T2000)
Impact Centre, 12-18 Hoxton Street, London N1 6NG
Tel: 020 7613 0743 Fax: 020 7613 5280
Email: transport2000@transport2000.demon.co.uk

T2000 is a national pressure group working solely on transport. It recently published *Changing Journeys To Work* (on green transport plans), and a similar document aimed at the NHS – *Healthy Transport Toolkit*. Works on a wide range of policy measures, research and dissemination initiatives with regard to reducing business and commuter travel.

TravelWise
The Secretary, National TravelWise, Lancashire County Council, Environment Directorate, Guild House, Cross Street Preston, Lancashire PR1 8RD
Tel: 01772 263649 Fax: 01772 263649
Email: 101472.22@compuserve.com
Website: www.travelwisenet.com, with link to SPIN (Seamless Passenger Information Network)
www.pti.org.uk

A national association of around 80 local authorities. Started in Hertfordshire, but is now adopting a national structure, with regional groups and a website

Further information

Publications

Changing Journeys to Work – an employer's guide to green commuter plans 1997. Published by T2000.
ISBN 0 907347 44 4. £30.00.

Company cars 1995 T2000. Available from T2000 – 020 7388 8386. £2.00.

Cycle friendly infrastructure – guidelines for planning and design 1996 DETR, Bicycle Association, Cyclists' Touring Club and The Institute of Highways & Transportation. ISBN 0 90223717 9. £15.00.

Energy Savings Through Improved Driver Training. Department of the Environment Good Practice Case Study 311. Available from ETSU, which manages the DETR's Energy Efficiency Best Practice Programme.

Fuel Consumption in Freight Haulage Fleets. Energy Consumption Guide 59.

Fuel Management for Transport Operators. Department of the Environment Good Practice Case Study 342.

Getting the Prices Right: a European scheme for making transport pay its true costs. 1993. European Federation for Transport and the Environment. Available from T2000 – Tel: 020 7388 8386.

Motor Vehicle Pollution: reduction strategies beyond 2010. 1995. Organisation for Economic Co-operation and Development. ISBN 9 26414312 2. £20. Available from The Stationery Office Ltd.

Moving Forward – a UNISON policy statement on public transport. UNISON ISBN 0 904198 13 8. £3.00 (free to UNISON members).

National Cycling Strategy 1996 DETR, Driver Information & Traffic Management Division.

A New Deal for Transport Better for Everyone – The Government's White Paper on the future of transport DETR. Published by The Stationery Office Limited. ISBN 0 10139502 7. £16.50

Preparing Your Organisation for Transport in the Future: the benefits of green transport plans, DETR, free.

Staff Travel – good practice 1998. Published by Cheshire County Council. Available from Jamie Matthews, TravelWise Team, County Hall, Chester, Cheshire CH1 1SF. Tel: 01244 603996 Fax: 01244 603958.

Traffic Advisory Leaflet 11/97 – Cycling to Work 1997 DETR, Driver Information & Traffic Management Division.

Websites

CAMPARIE
www.camparie.com/ (European projects to assess effectiveness of travel awareness campaigns)

Carsharing
www.ecoplan.org./carshare (Carsharing projects around the world, links to relevant websites, email contact lists, library and software information)

ELTIS
www.eltis.org (Limited information on European local transport projects)

Organisations

Department of the Environment, Transport and the Regions
Free Literature: Fax: 0870 1226 237

Websites:
www.detr.gov.uk./
(transport policy documentation)

www.local-transport.detr.gov.uk/ index.htm
(green transport plans)

www.local-transport.detr.gov.uk/schooltravel
(school transport plans)

Energy Efficiency Enquiries Bureau
ETSU, Harwell, Didcot, Oxfordshire, OX11 0RA
Tel: 01235 436747 Fax: 01235 432390
Website: www.etsu.com

4 Our homes and where we live – the built environment

Introduction

THE BUILT ENVIRONMENT – towns and cities – is where most people live in the UK. In many ways it is a problematic part of the environment, yet if we are to improve quality of life across the UK, making the built environment a better place to be is an essential issue for sustainable communities. It is estimated that about half the world's fossil fuel use is related to the servicing of buildings: this means that 50% of the world's CO2 outputs are under the control of designers and inhabitants of buildings.

The built environment can be broadly broken down into four related aspects:

- the buildings where we live, work and relax – their design and construction
- the open spaces around those buildings
- the neighbourhoods which those buildings make up
- the towns and cities themselves.

It is also important to consider the built environment in relation to the countryside and open spaces around it, and in terms of how people move around within it. This is crucial in the light of Government forecasts suggesting that 4.4 million new households may form in England by 2016. Much of this growth will be because young people are leaving home earlier, more people are getting divorced and people are living longer. The question of how and where these people will be housed is one of the most important environmental and social issues of the decade.

● Sustainable towns and cities

Making our towns and cities more sustainable is a long-term job. It is also essential – cities are where most of us live, work and relax, and they are centres for all sorts of economic activity. Much of this involves spatial planning – working out what is needed where, and how different parts of a town relate to each other. Local authorities have a key role to play in this work, through the production of development plans. But there are many other bodies involved in work at this level that can also provide advice and assistance.

The shape and structure of a sustainable town or city has long been discussed and disputed, with some groups calling for high density compact cities, where walking, cycling and public transport are chosen methods of transport, but where there may be less open space. Conversely the 'garden cities' movement launched in the early 20th century believed in integrating green space into cities. Both ideas now face new challenges from car-focused developments such as out-of-town and urban fringe offices and shopping centres.

New approaches are now being developed, such as low impact settlements or transit-oriented developments (based around public transport nodes) as it becomes clear that the impact of towns and cities is not just about what happens in the immediate area, but is also about wider issues, notably the resources used, the waste generated, the work that is done there, and how people travel in and between conurbations. In effect each city has a 'footprint' much greater than the actual area it covers: it has been suggested that London uses an area 125 times greater than the city simply to produce food and forest products and to absorb the carbon dioxide produced as London goes about its work.

New pressures, new solutions?

The big questions for our cities is simple: where will the new housing go? There is now widespread concern about the environmental implications of greenfield house building. As people leave the cities and move into surburbs and rural areas, pressures increase on previously greenfield sites for housing and related services, and inner-city economies are weakened. Research published by the Joseph Rowntree Foundation (May 1999) warns that the revival of Britain's cities is being threatened by 'abandoned neighbourhoods' where the demand for housing has collapsed. Manchester and Newcastle have lost a fifth of their population in less than 40 years.

In response to the prolonged debate in the media over greenfield house-building, the Labour Government has begun to promote urban renewal. In February 1998, it published *Planning for the Communities of the Future*, a policy statement on housing and land-use policy. This set out proposals to 'help us achieve our twin aims of an urban renaissance and of ensuring a green and pleasant land we can hand on to future generations.'

Lauded as the most significant step was the target for using brownfield sites; new policies should allow 'local planning authorities to be able to raise the national proportion of new homes to be built on previously developed land to 60% over the next ten years'. *Planning for the Communities of the Future* makes a welcome reference to 'social housing' as well as the expected 'affordable housing' but these problems along with those of balancing greenfield and brownfield sites are still a long way from sustainable solutions.

The Government's Select Committee on the Environment, Transport and Regional Affairs also published its report on housing in July 1998. One of the key recommendations was that most new homes should be built in surburban areas on brownfield land or in converted buildings, and that the provision of greenfield sites for development must be severely restricted. Shelter, the national housing campaign, also stressed in its 1998 report *An urban and rural renaissance* that there is no need to destroy the countryside by building on greenfield land to provide houses for homeless people and those in bad housing.

It is also important to remember that, while cities may be exciting places to live in, for the poor and excluded they can be dangerous and frightening. Cities are very inequitable, with the poorest often living within a mile of the richest. While everyone may suffer from air pollution in cities, it has been shown usually to be worst in poorest areas, which are often those around major arterial roads.

Making it happen – an 'urban renaissance'?

Trying to solve the problems of cities can be a daunting task: issues such as housing, employment, environment and transport are linked in ways that seem inextricable. What the UN describes as 'the quest for the sustainable city' will be a long and hard one. Nevertheless much good work is being done.

In the UK the Government's Urban Task Force is calling for an 'Urban Renaissance'. Its recent report identifies many positive steps that can be and are being taken, and calls for a new Government White Paper on urban policy. More practically it sets out ten key objectives for urban policy up to 2021. The first of these is encouraging: that 'all urban neighbourhoods will be managed according to principles of sustainable development', although the same objective then talks solely of 'environmental' indicators. It also stresses that public services should specifically address 'the needs and aspirations of urban communities' and that all urban areas should be managed 'according to standards agreed by the local community'.

The real question of course is 'will (and how will) it actually happen?'. It's a long way from our current city structures to this bright new vision and the current links between vision and reality are not clear. But good work is being done: much of it is emerging through urban regeneration programmes, but also through initiatives such as Local Agenda 21 and the work done by the UN Centre for Human Settlements through its Habitat programme.

KEY LINKAGES:
Other relevant sections of this guide are: almost all of it! – sustainable towns and cities are where all these issues come together.

Key organisations

The Civic Trust
17 Carlton House Terrace, London SW1Y 5AW
Tel: 020 7930 0914 Fax: 020 7321 0180
Email: pride@civictrust.org.uk
Website: www.civictrust.org.uk

Works to bring about a British urban renaissance, seeks to involve local people in partnerships and applies sustainability principles to regeneration projects.

Council for the Protection of Rural England (CPRE)
(see Environmental organisations)

Planning Aid for London
Tel: 020 7613 4435 Fax: 020 7613 4452
Email: pafl@demon.co.uk

PAL provides free and independent town planning advice to community groups, and can advise groups outside London on their best local advice point.

Royal Town Planning Institute (RTPI)
26 Portland Place, London W1N 4BE
Tel: 020 7636 9107 Fax: 020 7323 1582
Email: d_rose@policy.rtpi.co.uk

RTPI is the official body responsible for maintaining standards of professional competence and conduct for planners. It promotes the role of planners and presents their views on policy issues. RTPI has branches in Scotland and N Ireland and has a weekly publication, *Planning* which covers all current planning issues:
Tel: 020 8845 8545 Website: www.planning.haynet.com

Town and Country Planning Association (TCPA)
17 Carlton House Terrace, London SW1Y 5AW
Tel: 020 7930 8903 Fax: 020 7930 3280
Website: www.tcpa.org.uk

TCPA campaigns for the reform of the UK planning system to make it more responsive to people's needs and aspirations and to promote sustainable development. Publishes a monthly magazine on planning and environmental issues.

Urban Forum
4 Dean's Ct, St Paul's Churchyard, London EC4V 5AA
Tel: 020 7248 3111 Fax: 020 7248 3222
Email: info@urbanforum.org.uk
Website: www.urbanforum.org.uk

The Forum is an umbrella body for urban and regional policy, with particular regard to regeneration issues. It links the voluntary sector to the government. It runs an information service for members and a newsletter, Urban Clearway.

Women's Design Service (WDS)
52 Featherstone Street, London EC1Y 8RT
Tel: 020 7490 5210 Fax: 020 7490 5212
Website: www.wds.org.uk

WDS works with women in the urban environment on community safety, regeneration, access and policy.

Homes and buildings

Theory and practice for green and more sustainable buildings has advanced enormously over the last few years. Any architect, builder or designer working on new buildings or refurbishing old ones has a wealth of material and advice to draw on.

For many people green buildings are still just a dream: there are millions in the UK who are living in sub-standard housing, in short-term or bed and breakfast accommodation, or who are homeless. As well as the immediate and traumatic problems, it should be obvious that people forced to live in such situations are likely to be alienated and disempowered, and excluded from community-level action. While this is a huge problem, there are still tens of thousands of empty homes across the UK. Bringing these buildings back into use and perhaps also converting unused office or light industrial buildings into homes could transform this problem (see 'The neighbourhoods', below).

Government policy aims for a decent home to be within the reach of every household. This will not be easy – it is estimated that about 40% of the people in the predicted rise in new households by 2016 will not be able to afford housing at current market prices. Expanding the availability and choice of rented housing is therefore crucial, which will mean:

- encouraging the growth of private rented housing, thereby bringing empty properties back into use
- promoting efficient management of social housing stock
- providing Government funding for housing associations to build new homes or convert existing buildings
- targeting financial support on individual households so they can rent privately.

People need more than homes: they need homes that are safe, and homes that they can afford to heat. Affordable warmth (see 'Energy use' in section 2) should go with affordable homes. There are many initiatives aimed at improving the quality of housing stock: these include tenants' campaigns aimed at finding workable solutions to the effects of dampness, lack of insulation and the costs of heating, and the work of organisations such as Heatwise in Glasgow who aim to improve the fabric of existing property in order to improve dryness, warmth and costs while also providing local employment.

Energy use in homes accounts for 30% of the UK's total energy consumption, so there are also global issues. Re-designing our living and working spaces to demonstrate the viability of sustainable principles in action is the idea behind many exciting new initiatives across the UK. The Sherwood Energy Village in Nottinghamshire links super-insulated typical housing with renewable energy features, while the Hockerton Housing Project is the UK's first earth-sheltered, self-sufficient ecological housing development. The five houses are the centre of a sustainable development using minimal energy and with little environmental impact. There is however a long way to go before these new ideas become common practice.

In the longer term renewable energy is likely to be integrated into housing. The Government has recognised that solar energy has real potential. It is now seeking industry's involvement in taking forward three major new initiatives in the field, including a field trial of around 100 homes across the country to test photovoltaic installations under day-to-day conditions.

KEY LINKAGES:
Other relevant sections of this guide are:
Energy, Poverty

Key organisations

Association for Environment Conscious Building (AECB)
Nant-y-Garreg, Saron, Llandysul, Carmarthenshire SA44 5EJ Tel/Fax: 01599 370908
Email: buildgreen@aol.com
Website: http://members.aol.com/buildgreen

AECB is the leading independent environmental building trade organisation in the UK. It supports environmentally responsible practices within building by promoting the use of safe, healthy and sustainable materials, and encouraging innovation. It publishes a quarterly magazine *Building for a Future*, a Network newsletter for members and a directory of products and services, *Greener Building*.

The Building Research Establishment (BRE)
(see Main organisations)

BRE has a wealth of information on green buildings and runs the Energy Efficiency Best Practice Programme, which includes good practice case studies and information on low energy housing.

Centre for Alternative Technology
(see Main organisations)

Community Architecture Group
A network of community architects working to set up an independent charity to promote community-focused work and to run a Community Projects Fund to support it. For more information contact Judith Marshall Tel: 020 7336 7777 Email: ptea@demon.co.uk

Construction Resources Centre
16 Great Guildford Street, London SE1 0HS
Tel: 020 7450 2211 Fax: 020 7450 2212
Email: info@ecoconstruct.com
Website: www.ecoconstruct.com

The UK's first ecological builders' merchants and building centre, with a huge range of materials on display and for sale.

Ecological Design Association
British School, Slad Road, Stroud, Glos GL5 1QW
Tel: 01453 765575 Fax: 01453 759211

Promotes and advises on green design for buildings and products. Produces the *EcoDesign* journal and a members' newsletter. There is also a Scottish branch.

Shelter
88 Old Street, London EC1V 9HU
Tel: 0171 505 2000 Fax: 0171 505 2169

Shelter campaigns for decent homes that everyone can afford. It provides advice and assistance to people in housing need.

● The open spaces

Urban Nature has become an increasingly important area of work. It includes what we do with gardens, allotments, community gardens and city farms, with parks and recreation grounds, with uncared-for 'intermediate space' around housing developments, roads, and public buildings, and with the few sites of special importance, such as nature reserves, that are still found in every conurbation.

More than ever, green space is under threat in towns and cities. The pressure for new housing and new workspaces, at a time when protection of the countryside around cities is becoming a key issue, means that almost any open space may be viewed as potential development land. This has in turn led in some cases to conflicts between those seeking to protect urban open space and those working to save green belts.

It is vital that such conflicts are resolved and joint strategies developed that focus more on the re-use of unwanted and derelict buildings rather than on the easy option of building on open space. Groups such as 'The Land is Ours' have undertaken direct action to highlight the scandal of unused land in cities, while work done for Friends of the Earth suggests that 75% of the new housing that will be needed could be built in urban areas.

At the same time there has been an upsurge of interest in urban spaces, especially for community gardens and food growing. While some bodies have resisted this, citing concerns about land contamination, current research suggests that there are huge opportunities for growing far more food in our cities. There are also new initiatives to 'green' tower blocks and large estates. English Nature has also produced valuable material on green spaces in towns and cities.

KEY LINKAGES:
Other relevant sections of this guide are:
Biodiversity, Food

Key organisations

Allotments Coalition Trust
(see Food)

Federation of City Farms and Community Gardens (see Food)

Groundwork (see Main organisations)

Shell Better Britain Campaign
(see Main organisations)

Urban Wildlife Partnership (UWP)
The Kiln, Mather Road, Newark, Notts NG24 1WT
Tel: 01636 677 711 Fax: 01636 511616
Email: info@wildlife-trusts@cix.co.uk

UWP links and supports the growing number of urban wildlife groups of all types that work to create a better future for wildlife in towns and cities.

Further information

English Nature research reports Nos. 153 and 256 on greenspaces and green networks in towns and cities.

● The neighbourhoods

Dealing with problems at a neighbourhood level is at the core of work for more sustainable communities. The importance of working on solutions that improve a whole neighbourhood has long been acknowledged in areas with high levels of poverty and exclusion – regeneration strategies now recognise this and the importance of involving local people in drawing up and implementing plans to improve their neighbourhoods.

This work also relates directly to the buildings, especially in council- or housing association-built estates where the building will share common features and problems. Organisations such as Neighbourhood Energy Action have pioneered work in this field. More ambitiously, the Sustainable Urban Neighbourhood (SUN) Initiative set up and managed by the URBED group is seeking to draw all these issues together and is looking at what our neighbourhoods might look like and how they will work in a more sustainable society.

Improving neighbourhoods clearly isn't just about the built environment – improving the local environment and community safety work are essential parts of any neighbourhood strategy (see other parts of this guide). It is also about getting the neighbourhoods busy and active: one problem here is the high levels of empty homes – something the Empty Homes Agency and its community campaign has been set up to try and deal with.

One of the main problems for 'undesirable' neighbourhoods is that people move away. This leads to housing becoming derelict, vandalism and a spiral of decline. There are large estates in parts of England and Scotland where councils cannot persuade people to live: it has been suggested that some newly renovated estates may simply be knocked down, since they are so unpopular.

Getting people to take pride in where they live needs outside support and investment, both to improve the local economy and the housing, but also to make the area an attractive and safe place to live. Research by the Joseph Rowntree Foundation has shown how important it is to understand disadvantaged neighbourhoods, including their histories and their assets as well as their problems. It stresses the need to 'bring residents to the centre of regeneration', and that this needs national as well as local commitment.

While 'inner-city' areas have tended to be the focus of much work on urban sustainability, most people actually live in areas that can best be described as 'suburban'. There has been much less focus on suburban areas, but many show signs of stress, with declining local centres, deteriorating community facilities and dependence on cars. The more widespread nature of such communities makes wholesale regeneration and rebuilding much harder. Creating sustainable suburbs may be one of the biggest challenges of all, and one where national support for locally-based initiatives that suit local needs will be more important than ever.

Not all neighbourhoods have big problems, but people everywhere would like to see improvements. Working out how to improve the local surroundings had been at the core of many programmes such as community profiling or 'parish mapping' (pioneered by Common Ground). Such programmes focus on working out not just what people wish to improve but also what they value and celebrate.

It's sometimes hard to know what makes a particular town or neighbourhood an attractive place to live: finding and identifying such a 'sense of place' may be at the heart of developing more sustainable cities.

KEY LINKAGES:
Other relevant sections of this guide are:
Safe environments and all material on
Strong communities

Key organisations

Common Ground (see Main organisations)

Community Development Foundation
(see Main organisations)
Produces a valuable guide to Single Regeneration Budget (SRB) Guidelines and Procedures.

The Empty Homes Agency
195–197 Victoria Street, London SW1E 5NE
Tel: 020 7828 6288   Email: eha@mcmail.com
EHA is an independent charity, set up in 1992 to tackle the problem of England's 700,000 empty homes, while precious greenfield sites are threatened by development. It works with individual owners and larger organisations to bring homes back into use. It is also encouraging local authorities to establish empty property strategies – a bottom-up, grassroots campaign – and has set up the Community Action on Empty Homes programme.

Neighbourhood Initiatives Foundation (NIF)
The Poplars, Lightmoor, Telford, Shropshire TF4 3QN
Tel: 01952 590777   Fax: 01952 591771
Email: nif@cableinet.co.uk   Website: www.nif.co.uk
NIF works to involve residents of neighbourhoods in identifying and realising the needs of their communities. It produces a range of materials and provides training, including running 'Planning for Real' sessions (a registered trademark of NIF). Its website carries the newsletter, 'Planning for Real' publications, membership and training details.

Tenants Participation Advisory Service for England (TPAS)
Brunswick House, Broad Street, Salford M6 5BZ
Tel: 0161 745 7903   Fax: 0171 745 9259
Email: info@tpas.org.uk   Website: www.tpas.org.uk
TPAS works to develop the involvement of tenants in managing their housing, runs training and events, and provides advice and consultancy. Membership is open to any tenants group or association.

URBED
41 Old Birley Street, Hulme, Manchester M15 5RF
Tel: 0161 226 5078   Fax: 0161 226 7307
Email: sun@urbed.co.uk
Website: www.urbed.co.uk/sun/
URBED is an architecture and urban design consultancy which runs the Sustainable Urban Neighbourhood (SUN) Initiative (with other partners) and many other projects. The SUN project produces a good free newsletter *SUNdial*, which covers many aspects of sustainable city work.

Further information

Joseph Rowntree Foundation
The Homestead, 40 Water End, York YO30 6WP
Tel: 01904 629241, Publications: 01904 615905
Fax: 01904 620072 Website: www.jrf.org.uk

The Joseph Rowntree Foundation is an independent research body that focuses on the built environment. It has a great many publications and produces short summaries of each, entitled *Findings*. Full details of all these are available on its website.

Publications

Anybody Home? Empty Homes and their environmental consequences CPRE 1998 Looks at how re-using empty homes could negate the need to build on greenfield sites. £2.50. ISBN 0 94604491 0.

Building a Sustainable Future – homes for an autonomous community. DETR/Energy Efficiency Best Practice Programme. October 1998. Available from BRE This publication represents one vision of the factors likely to contribute to sustainability at a community scale, with ideas on the layout, density and transport considerations in settlement design.

Building the 21st Century Home. David Rudlin and Nicholas Falk (of URBED). £19.99. Architectural Press, 1999.

But would you live there? Shaping attitudes to urban living. A report on public attitudes by URBED and MORI, summary available from DETR Free Literature.

Joined Up Thinking – a directory of good practice for local authority empty property strategies. Empty Homes Agency. £8.50 including postage.

Planning for a Sustainable Environment. Andrew Blowers (editor) Earthscan, 1993.

Regeneration and Sustainable Communities. Gabriel Chanan and Alison West, Community Development Foundation, 1999.

The Slow Death of Great Cities? Urban abandonment or urban renaissance. Anne Power & Katherine Mumford, Joseph Rowntree Foundation. May 1999. Free summary available from JRF, 64 Hallfield Road, Layerthorpe, York YO31 7SW Tel: 01904 430033.

Towards an Urban Renaissance. The final report of the Urban Task Force London 1999 £19.99 Published by E&F Spon, tel: 01264 343071. A free summary is available from the DETR Free Literature office (see Main organisations) or on the DETR website.

Sustainable livelihoods

Introduction

FOR BILLIONS OF PEOPLE AROUND THE WORLD 'earning a living' is just that: bringing in enough money and resources to keep themselves and their families alive. It's not so long ago that in the UK the way out of poverty was simple: get a job. Now things are different. Full employment – 'jobs for everyone' – has become little more than a dream, and too often the jobs have no security or prospects, while even the minimum wage is hardly enough to keep a family out of the poverty trap.

For some the 'new flexibility' in employment is a challenge and an opportunity: to others it is just another problem. But for everyone it is reality, and more and more ways to cope are emerging. For many poor communities this is nothing new: shared child care, shared resources and mutual support are a simple fact of life. Dionisia Acosta, an activist in the Dominican Republic summed it up: 'We, the poor, have to organise because we have no alternative. The poor must help the poor and hope that society will change.'

Agenda 21 recognises this: in Chapter 5, on combating poverty, the first objective is to enable 'all people to achieve sustainable livelihoods'. Livelihood may involve jobs but it can also involve voluntary work, local trading schemes and, above all, access to the services that people need at as low a cost as possible. Governments may set up programmes to combat social exclusion, individuals can play their parts, but effective action will need strong local programmes to deliver service and support, and that can help people take control of their own lives.

● Strong and sustainable local economies

Much of Agenda 21 is quite simply about how to make economic systems sustainable. Yet those negotiating the text lacked clear ideas of how sustainable economics might work – beyond their expressed determination to get access to better indicators of success than just money. So Agenda 21 sets out ways that we can monitor the world better, to know whether things are getting better or worse. That goal lies at the heart of sustainable economics as it has developed since then.

Conventional economics is partially blind. It draws a circle around the financial economy, and cannot see outside it to incorporate social or environmental issues. 'Success' is simply about money with a very narrow interpretation of what wealth is. Real 'wealth', say the sustainable economists, goes way beyond money. It includes the state of the planet, but also the love, happiness, families and community without which we would be extremely poor.

> **KEY LINKAGES:**
> *Other relevant sections of this guide are:*
> *Strong communities, Poverty*

Current issues

If we are to develop more sustainable economies, both nationally and locally, there is a range of issues to be tackled.

Developing alternative indicators

The first step for a sustainable economy is to measure success more broadly, which is why cities and towns across the world have been developing their own alternative economic indicators to measure what people really think is important. They are usually agreed between people and the local council, and they make it possible to measure progress towards the kind of goals people want – rather than just narrow measures of money and debt. Indicators include empty homes (Dundee), cars with one occupant (Peterborough), distance to leisure facilities (Greenwich), ponds with newts and frogs (Oldham), and even breeding golden eagles (Strathclyde).

The Government has now published its own sustainability indicators, which – although its choices remain controversial – will allow us to measure its progress against more than just old-fashioned Gross National Product.

Green taxation policies

A decade ago the idea of shifting taxes off the things we want – jobs and value – and putting them onto pollution or energy waste, was a fringe idea. Now it is being studied by every government in the world, and is already being put into effect, even in Britain.

Britain started by taxing landfill as a way of discouraging waste, and other green taxes may be on the way, thanks to recent backing from a Treasury committee. Strictly speaking, green taxes need not be additional, but as a replacement for the kind of taxes which are currently discouraging companies from taking on staff. It is also crucial that green taxes do not have a disproportionate impact on poorer communities.

Social auditing and accounting

Every company has a bottom line, but usually it is just a simple record of profit and loss. But as organisations increasingly realise they owe a duty, not just to shareholders, but also to other stakeholders – customers, staff, suppliers, the local community – their success or failure in this should also be measured.

Companies like Body Shop and Ben & Jerry's ice cream led the way in this 'social auditing'. Others, like Levi Strauss, have been experimenting with codes of practice about how they treat the people around the world who supply them. Now the Government is backing the Ethical Trading Initiative, which is looking at ways of extending these experiments and developing the best ways of making sure the impact of companies is measured.

Community banks

All over the UK banks have been closing branches. Almost 10% of the population is without bank accounts – even though it is difficult to get a job without one. And while money pours into overblown property markets in some places, it is almost impossible to get a mortgage in others – or raise money for a small business.

A new generation of credit unions and community financial institutions is emerging on both sides of the Atlantic, able to lend small amounts to people who need them and to funnel loans to local projects.

In the USA, the Community Reinvestment Act forces banks to reveal where they are lending money. This has been able to leverage over $350 billion in new finance for affordable housing in disadvantaged areas.

Ethical investment

Individual action is also important. Every purchase we make is a vote for the kind of world we want. Investors are increasingly putting their money where their values are – making sure it is invested in ways that really make us 'wealthier'. Over £2 billion is now invested ethically in Britain, and considerably more in the USA – all of it screened against ethical or environmental criteria. Over 85% of big corporations have also taken to relating their marketing to a cause, in an attempt to improve their reputations.

Major investors can also have a big impact if they start to adopt ethical criteria. A number of local authorities have looked hard at where their pension funds are invested and are discovering that it is possible to combine good returns with ethical criteria – Nottinghamshire is one that is leading the way. This should be a priority for all authorities seeking to develop their Local Agenda 21 programmes.

The latest research shows that there are 15 FTSE 100 companies in the UK which have more than 5% of their shares owned by ethical investors. This is a powerful new position for the ethical investment sector, and all sides are only now coming to terms with the implications.

Local currencies

LETS currencies are Local Exchange Trading Schemes, and are the biggest success story for the 'new economics'. A few years ago LETS schemes were seen very much as an 'alternative', appealing mainly to green enthusiasts. Now things have changed and the value of LETS to poor communities is recognised.

LETS help communities survive economically when they are running out of cash. They mean that people can afford to buy the goods and services they need, not with money, but with an agreed local currency, which puts people's needs in touch with others who can fulfil them. Almost half the cities in Britain have got involved in setting up local currencies to take the edge off local poverty – and provide a means whereby people without jobs can rebuild their communities and regain their self-esteem.

Time money, similar to LETS, but paid to people who help out in their community, has also recently arrived in the UK, as an important new tool for rebuilding the local wealth' – what the government calls 'social capital' – which underpins communities and allows them to thrive.

Local currencies like time dollars from the USA help to rediscover that we can use people's skills and time, by redefining work in terms of what needs to be done rather than that much narrower range of services the market is prepared to pay for. Other local currencies, like LETS or hours – the printed notes which began in Ithaca in the USA can keep money circulating locally, encouraging local production and benefiting local trade at the expense of distant multinationals.

International perspectives

The biggest challenge for sustainable development at the international level is to find the money and resources for sustainability programmes. If richer nations fail to come up with money to help poorer nations then the goals in Agenda 21 are unlikely to be met.

Such financing could eventually come from new sources of global taxation, either on air fuel or on international currency speculation, at least 95% of which has nothing to do with facilitating trade. This proposal – the so-called Tobin Tax – would have the added benefit of calming the world markets, which are now perceived as a source of serious unsustainability.

Current issues in the UK

The Government still has a long way to go to embrace environmental taxes fully and to link them directly with tackling social exclusion. Taxes on quarrying, incineration, greenfield development and pesticides have all been proposed.

There is increasing recognition that environmental regulation can not only improve the planet, but can also result in innovation and jobs – for example by developing Britain's fledgling renewable energy industry. The landfill tax is encouraging an energetic new recycling sector by providing an incentive to organisations to be careful what they throw away.

The idea of sustainability is increasingly linking environment and social exclusion, and a number of ideas of sustainable economies have been adopted by the Government's Social Exclusion Unit, and gathered in the Unit's recent report *Bringing People Together*.

Like so many other aspects of sustainability, there are important actions which governments and businesses must take. But individuals also have an important part to play – even if it is just joining their local currency scheme, getting organic vegetables delivered to their door, and keeping a careful check that their money is invested in ways that are building sustainability, not undermining it.

Key organisations

Baratraria Foundation
Keeper's Cottage, Pitlandie, Perth PH1 3HZ
Tel: 01738 582232 Email: rutha@baratraria.org

Works to support sustainable community development, and to implement the new Scottish Organisational Currency System with help from the European Commission.

British Association for Fair Trade Shops
c/o Gateway World Shop, Market Place, Durham DH1 3NJ Tel: 0191 384 7173 Fax: 0191 375 0729

This is a network of independent retail shops whose aims are to promote fair trade and make it work in the UK.

Business in the Community
44 Baker Street, London W1M 1DH
Tel: 020 7224 1600 Fax: 020 7486 1700
Website: www.bitc.org.uk

BITC is among the leaders in the corporate responsibility field, and also supports Business in the Environment.

Charity Logistics
Camelford House, 87–89 Albert Embankment, London SE1 7FP Tel: 020 7582 8800
Fax: 020 7882 8859 Website: www.charityvfree, see also www.cybercycle.org

A project that provides training by recycling computers which would otherwise go into landfill.

Ethical Investment Research Service (EIRIS)
80–84 Bondway, London SW8 1SF Tel: 020 7840 5700

EIRIS provides information to ethical investors and helps build what is now the second fastest growing financial services sector.

Fair Shares
Resource Centre, City Works, Alfred Street, Gloucester
Tel: 01452 541337 Email: fairshares@cablenet.co.uk
Website: www.fairshares.org

Introducing the idea of time dollars to the UK, with nine linked time money projects in Gloucestershire.

Forum for the Future
227a City Road, London EC1V 1JT
Tel: 020 7477 7707 Fax: 020 7251 6268
Email: l.harding@forum-for-the-future.org.uk

Forum for the Future has a Local Economy Unit working on economic issues with local authorities.

Jubilee 2000 Coalition
PO Box 100, London SE1 7RT Tel: 020 7739 1000
Fax: 020 7739 2300 Website: www.jubilee2000uk.org

Organisers of the massive campaign to cancel Third World Debt.

LETSlink UK
2 Kent Street, Portsea, Portsmouth PO1 3BS
Tel: 01705 730639 Fax: 01705 730629
Email: liz@letslink.demon.co.uk
Website: www.LETSlinkUK.demon.co.uk

Promotes the idea of LETS local currencies around the UK, and negotiates with the Government to end the benefits anomaly that may exclude the very people it would benefit most.

New Economics Foundation (see Main organisations)
Cinnamon House, 6–8 Cole Street, London SE1 4YH
Tel: 020 7407 7447 Fax: 020 7407 6473
Email: info@neweconomics.org
Website: www.neweconomics.org

NEF arose out of The Other Economic Summit (TOES), which first met in London in 1984 and now meets around the world parallel to the G7 summit. It specialises in local indicators, local money, social auditing, participation and community banking.

Further information

Publications

After the Crash: the emergence of the rainbow economy, Guy Dauncey, Greenprint, £6.99

Bringing People Together: a national strategy for neighbourhood renewal, Social Exclusion Unit. Cabinet Office, £9.50.

Communities Count! A step-by-step guide to community sustainability indicators. Published by New Economics Foundation. £15 institutions, £10 individuals.

Community Works! A guide to community economic action, published by New Economics Foundation. £3.

Funny Money: in search of alternative cash, by David Boyle, published by Harper Collins. £14.99. Website: oneworld.compuserve.com/hornepages/dcboyle

Future Wealth: a new economics for the 21st century, James Robertson, Cassell.

Getting the Best Out of Indicators – the government's response to the UK Round table on Sustainable Development, free from the DETR.

LETS Act Locally – The growth of Local Exchange Trading Schemes, Jonathan Croall, Gulbenkian Foundation, £8.

Short Circuit: strengthening local economies for security in an unstable world, Richard Douthwaite, Green Books, £14.95.

Small is Bankable: community reinvestment in the UK, published by Joseph Rowntree Foundation. £11.95. Website: www.jrf.org.uk

The New Economy – a comprehensive CD-ROM containing huge amounts of information on all these issues. Published winter 1999 by the New Economics Foundation.

● Poverty

'There can be no higher purpose than working to eradicate poverty and promote sustainable development in the world's poorest countries.'

Tony Blair, April 1997

There are now 12 million people living in poverty in the UK (25% of the population). This is well over double the number in 1979 – 5 million. (UK Report to the Commission on Sustainable Development – Section on Poverty, 1994)

Poverty and sustainable development

The 1992 Rio Earth Summit made the links between poverty and environment issues in Agenda 21. Chapter 3 of that document spells it out very clearly: 'A specific anti-poverty strategy is one of the basic conditions for ensuring sustainable development.' Yet despite a lot of talk, there has so far been little action within the UK to link this 'basic condition' with other sustainability issues. There are very few visions of 'sustainable communities' where poverty has been tackled and reduced or eradicated.

The links between poverty and the environment are many and complex. They vary for different people and different organisations. The circular relationship of poor environments affecting poor people is more obvious in developing countries, where poverty can lead to environmental degradation, often through the cultivation of steep hillsides or felling of trees for fuel. Environmental mismanagement can also deprive whole communities of their traditional livelihoods.

In the UK the relationship is less direct. In inner cities poverty can degrade both the physical and social environment, making the area less attractive and drawing more people in the neighbourhood into the poverty trap. Poverty can also undermine the opportunities for community-based environmental action, primarily by cutting people's confidence, their willingness and ability to participate, and the time they have available to take action. It can also lead to alienation, which can manifest itself destructively as anti-social reaction.

KEY LINKAGES:
Other relevant sections of the Guide are: Strong communities, Environmental justice, The Local economy, Health, and Community safety.

Social exclusion and poverty in the UK

Social exclusion is a declared priority for this government. It provides a new perspective on poverty and is embodied in the European Community's 1984 definition of poverty, which is used by many agencies – 'the circumstances of persons, families and groups of persons whose resources (material, cultural and social) are so limited as to exclude them from the minimum acceptable way of life in the Member State in which they live.'

This provides a wider focus than merely looking at poverty, and a key lesson must be that improving the local environment is not an 'add-on': it is an essential part of rebuilding community spirit and encouraging those people benefiting from training and development programmes to stay in the area and help it improve. The focus for this approach is the Social Exclusion Unit, created to develop ways of bringing the poorest neighbourhoods back into the mainstream of society and regenerating communities.

The arrival of a Labour government has also given renewed impetus to groups working on poverty, producing calls for a national poverty strategy and annual publication of poverty statistics, something the Government has now agreed to. In the context of the latter there has been much work on indicators of poverty, emphasising what poverty means to those who are poor. These indicators have recognised that poverty is not simply a matter of income but, again, reflects the way people and communities become isolated from society. Much of this has echoed international activity such the United Nations Development Programme's 1997 Human Development Report on poverty and European Commission work on citizenship.

Poverty – the current situation

But whatever definition of poverty is used – and there are several – government statistics suggest the situation deteriorated sharply during the 1980s when the gap between rich and poor widened considerably and it has still to show much improvement.

The most recent Households Below Average Income (HBAI) figures – the closest the UK has to any sort of national poverty statistics – show that by the mid-1990s, 24% of the population was living at, or below, half the average income. Within all groups there has been an increase in poverty. Households with children, people who are unemployed, work part-time or are self-employed are increasingly vulnerable to poverty. The 1991 Census identified an estimated 190,920 households as 'multiply deprived' and 15,370 households as 'seriously deprived'.

The HBAI statistics also highlight a difference between groups in society and between regions. More than 40% of people in lone parent families were in the bottom fifth of the range of income and almost 30% of children as a whole were in the bottom fifth. The income distributions of people headed by a member of an ethnic minority group were skewed towards the lower end of the scale. People living in Wales and the north of England were also more likely to be in that lowest 20%.

An environment for everyone? – action on poverty and sustainability

At the Government level there is little, if any, specific linkage between poverty and sustainable development but tackling poverty and promoting sustainable development are intimately entwined, as Agenda 21 acknowledges. Addressing poverty on a long-term basis requires measures which are sustainable by being appropriate for both the local environment and resources. The differences in the official statistics between regions highlight the need for local initiatives within national policy.

Some Local Agenda 21 (LA21) projects have tackled these issues, but there is a great deal more to be done. Many LA21s find it difficult to build links between environmental and anti-poverty initiatives within local government. This is an area where leadership is badly needed, and there is also much that LA21 activity can do to enable the involvement of people from disadvantaged communities.

Environmental NGOs also have a great potential to open up their work to new audiences, a challenge that several are now facing up to. CDF's publication *An Environment for Everyone*, a review of the links between environment and exclusion, suggests how organisations working on environmental issues can do much more to involve disadvanatged groups. Direct linking of environment and disadvantage is leading to work on 'Environmental Justice' (see Section 6).

Some of the best practice in this field is coming from regeneration initiatives which have developed programmes that seek to give people confidence, work experience and self-help appropriate to local conditions so that they can in turn make a valuable contribution to local sustainability. A considered sustainable approach might involve seeking to involve local people in all aspects of developing and managing regeneration programmes, rather than focusing on bringing in finance from outside the area. Rebuilding the local economy, using the innovative ideas that have come from the sustainable development movement, must go alongside communtiy development to build people's confidence and self-respect.

Key organisations

There are a large number of organisations tackling poverty; those listed here are groups that have a national overview and can put you in touch with projects specific to a particular area.

Child Poverty Action Group (CPAG)
94 White Lion Street, London N1 9PF
Tel: 020 7837 7979 Fax: 020 7837 6414
Email: staff@cpag.demon.co.uk
Website under development.

CPAG promotes action for the relief of poverty, and activities include providing a national service of welfare benefits advice and training. It takes legal test cases to ensure poor families receive the benefits due to them, undertakes research on family poverty in the UK, develops policies on tackling poverty and co-ordinates welfare rights networks.

Church Action on Poverty (CAP)
Central Buildings, Oldham Street, Manchester M1 1JT
Tel: 0161 236 9321 Fax: 0161 237 5359
Email: churchaction@cwcom.net
Website: www.church-poverty.org.uk

CAP has a programme of educational work and campaigns on the extent and causes of poverty within a Christian context. It works at the local and national level to change public attitudes and policies to promote lasting solutions to the problem of poverty. Local groups are involved in practical projects to tackle poverty in ways appropriate to the locality.

Community Development Foundation
(see Main organisations)

European Anti-Poverty Network (EAPN)
205 Rue Belliard Bte 13, B-1040 Brussels, Belgium
Tel: 322 230 4455 Fax:- 322 230 9733
Email: eapn@euronet.be Website: www.epitelio.org/eapn

EAPN links anti-poverty groups across Europe and produces much valuable material and a newsletter.

European Anti-Poverty Network – England
138 Digbeth, Birmingham B5 6DR Tel: 0121 643 4343
Email: eapneng@netcomuk.co.uk

EAPN England is a network of voluntary and community organisations working collectively to influence policy in England, the UK and the EU. It has full and associate member schemes and produces a quarterly newsletter.

Help the Aged
St James' Walk, London EC1R 0BE
Tel: 020 7253 0253 Fax: 020 7250 4474
Website: www.hta.org.uk

Help the Aged aims to improve the quality of life for older people, particularly those who are frail, isolated or poor.

Local Government Anti-Poverty Unit (LGAPU)
Layden House, 76–86 Turnmill Street,
London EC1M 5LG Tel: 020 7296 6600
Email: socpol@idea.gov.uk Website: www.idea.gov.uk

LGAPU supports local authorities in their work on social exclusion, sharing information and working with individual authorities on practice development. It produces a newsletter, *Poverty matters* (subscription is £26/year).

Low Pay Unit
27–29 Amwell Street, London EC1R 1UN
Tel: 020 7713 7616 Fax: 020 7713 7581
Email: lowpayunit@aol.com

The Unit investigates and publicises low pay, poverty and related issues. It lobbies Government and publishes reports as well as providing a rights service for the general public and advisers.

National Association of Citizens Advice Bureaux (NACAB)
115–123 Pentonville Road, London N1 9LZ
Tel: 020 7833 2181 Fax: 020 7833 4371
Website: www. nacab.org.uk

Although NACAB's local offices are concerned with giving advice on a wide range of issues, much of their work is poverty-related and involves debt advice. As a result they are involved in community development work, preventive work on debt and work on policy issues.

Oxfam
274 Banbury Road, Oxford OX2 7DZ
Tel: 01865 311311 Fax: 01865 313101
Website: www.oxfam.org.uk

Oxfam set up its British anti-poverty programme in 1995. In partnership with local groups, Oxfam works to tackle powerlessness. It is working with the Government's Social Exclusion Unit to break down stereotypical and negative views of poverty. Projects now include supporting homeworkers, food poverty and community support as well as policy work.

The Poverty Alliance
162 Buchanan Street, Glasgow G1 2LL
Tel: 0141 353 0440 Fax: 0141 353 0686
Email: thepovertyalliance@compuserve.com

Poverty Alliance is a national organisation, co-funded by the Scottish Office, which promotes the development of an anti-poverty strategy for Scotland and works with local communities to identify needs and progress projects. It also has a particular interest in food security, and supports the Communities Against Poverty Network, which consists mainly of volunteer community activists.

Save the Children Fund
17 Grove Lane, London SE5 8RD Tel: 020 7703 5400
Fax: 020 7716 2378 Website: www.savethechildren.org.uk

SCF undertakes long-term development and prevention work to help children, families and communities become self-sufficient. In the UK it works particularly on education, promoting young people's views in policy debates and supporting various projects, including some for travellers.

Shelter
88 Old Street, London EC1V 9HU Tel: 020 7505 2000
Fax: 020 7505 2169 Website: www.shelter.org.uk

Shelter campaigns for decent homes that everyone can afford. It provides advice and assistance to people in housing need, and runs regional housing aid centres.

Wales Council for Voluntary Action
Llys Ifor, Crescent Road, Caerphilly CF83 1XL
Tel: 01222 855100 Fax: 01222 855101
Email: inquiries@wcva.co.uk

WCVA is an umbrella organisation for the voluntary sector in Wales, with contacts in charities and community groups working on poverty issues.

Welsh Anti-Poverty Network
c/o Jim Hynes (Secretary) 55 Ffordd Pentre,
Mold CH7 1UY Tel/Fax: 01352 700104

A network of groups across Wales tackling issues of poverty and social exclusion. It carries details of a range of local projects across Wales, with contacts in charities and community groups working on poverty issues.

UK Coalition Against Poverty
17 Grove Lane, London SE5 8RD
Tel: 020 7703 5400 Fax: 020 7793 7612

The Coalition is an alliance of more than 160 groups including charities, community groups and local authorities who are working for a National Poverty Eradication Strategy. The coalition is running the two-year Voices for Change project, with funding from the Joseph Rowntree Charitable Trust, which seeks to help communities participate in policy debate on poverty, and gives those communities training and support in networking and capacity-building.

Further information

Publications

An Environment for Everyone. Church, Cade & Grant 1998 CDF. A review of how disadvantaged groups can be supported to become more involved in environmental work. £4.95.

An Inclusive Society: strategies for tackling poverty. Carey Oppenheim (ed) London: Institute for Public Policy Research, 1998.

The **Breadline Britain** project has several publications including: David Gordon et al. *Breadline Britain in the 1990s.* University of Bristol, 1997; and Jonathan Bradshaw et al. *Perceptions of Poverty and Social Exclusion.* University of Bristol, 1998

Bringing People Together: a national strategy for neighbourhood renewal. London: The Social Exclusion Unit. The Stationery Office, 1998

Ethnic Minorities in Britain: diversities and disadvantage. London: Tariq Modood et al. Policy Studies Institute, 1997.

Income and Wealth: the latest evidence. John Hills, Joseph Rowntree Foundation, 1998

Monitoring Poverty and Social Exclusion: Labour's inheritance. Catherine Howarth, Peter Kenway, Guy Palmer, Cathy Street York: Joseph Rowntree Foundation, 1998.

Poverty: the facts. Carey Oppenheim and Lisa Harker. London: Child Poverty Action Group, 1996.

Poverty and Sustainable Development in Scotland was produced as a submission to the UN Commission on Sustainable Development by the Scottish Environmental Forum.

Social Exclusion and Economic Regeneration. Proceedings of the conference of January 29th 1997 at the University of Glamorgan. Published by the University of Glamorgan Regional Research Programme and the Institute of Welsh Affairs, 1997

Websites

Lothian Poverty Alliance is an example of how local organisations use the Web:
www.lothianapa.freeserve.co.uk/index.htm

NACAB's website has contact details for local groups: www.nacab.org.uk

Details of **Oxfam**'s UK poverty programme and specific projects are at:
www.oxfam.org.uk/oxfam_at_work.html

The **Scottish Poverty Information Unit**'s website has a mass of information and discussion on poverty issues with aim of making data easily accessible to community groups and voluntary organisations: spiu.gcal.ac.uk/home.html

6 Building stronger communities

Introduction

THE PREVIOUS SECTIONS OF THIS GUIDE have shown how local action everywhere is leading to small (and large) steps towards sustainability. But many local programmes and projects often lack the support, confidence and skills that they need to make their work as effective as they believe it could be. Good community projects don't just happen: they may be driven by an inspired community leader or 'social entrepreneur', but even the most dynamic individual needs support. And too often, when a project depends on one person, then the project collapses when that person can no longer take part.

In the same way 'strong communities' won't just happen. If we want to see more active and effective community action, that goal needs to be planned for and worked towards just as carefully as any other project. Two of the key areas of work to help achieve that goal are community development and ensuring that everyone in the community can participate effectively. This section also looks at how communities can get a fair deal and at work being done on 'environmental justice'.

● Community development

Community development is central to sustainable communities. With so many pressures on local communities leading to fragmentation and exclusion, building strong communities takes time and planning. Community development has evolved over the last 30 years to become a well-defined body of work, with an overall goal of seeking to help communities, and groups within communities, to function more effectively.

There is a thriving level of activity in most communities across the UK. Even the most deprived have many groups working to improve life for residents. At any time about 50% of all residents are either involved in some form of unpaid local activity or are benefiting from the activities of community groups.

Trying to define 'the community' in any more detail than 'the area of activity that lies beyond the family' is of course difficult. Community means different things to different people and for a truly sustainable community to develop it may be necessary to include within that community the other species of animals and plants that live in the area.

Community development has traditionally been closely linked with work on social exclusion and poverty. This is central to the work, and can help people be less poor by helping them get access to training and employment opportunities, to better childcare facilities, and to the support that can be provided by community-managed resources and centres. Community development also goes beyond this grassroots activity by attempting to identify and deal with the reasons why certain areas are excluded and disadvantaged and to solve these problems at a policy level.

The last few years have seen a coming together of groups working on community development and some of those working on environmental issues. This makes very good sense, not least because those living in the poorest areas also tend to have the worst environments (see 'Environmental justice'). Sustainability is a key aim of both movements, alongside strong traditions of grassroots organising. This has also led to an increased focus on regeneration initiatives, with those working on 'sustainable regeneration' seeking to ensure that Government-funded initiatives through the Single Regeneration Budget do involve people effectively, meet their needs, provide long-term and lasting solutions to local problems and genuinely improve and benefit the local environment.

Links between community action and environmental concern have also been given a new focus by Local Agenda 21 programmes, with the call for local councils to 'consult with their communities'. Agenda 21 itself stresses the need for policies and strategies that include 'increased local control of resources, local institution-strengthening and capacity-building and greater involvement of non-governmental organisations and local levels of government…'

In the next few years community development will also play a key role in improving local delivery of key services and in the development of community plans. It is suggested in the Government's *Modern Local Government* White Paper that every council should develop such a plan to identify how that council will meet environmental, social, and economic priorities for its area.

Key organisations

BASSAC (British Association of Settlements and Social Action Centres)
1st Floor, Winchester House, Cranmer Road, London SW9 6EJ Tel: 020 7735 1075 Fax: 020 7735 0840
Email: bassac@mcr1.poptel.org.uk

A network of multi-purpose local centres committed to helping local communities bring about social change, and links over 1000 projects in 84 centres. The national office provides support, information and training, represents local centres to government, and helps them to take joint action on national issues.

Community Action Network
Panton House, 25 Haymarket, London SW1Y 4EN
Tel: 020 7321 2244 Fax: 020 7839 7414
Website: www.can-online.org.uk

Community Development Foundation
60 Highbury Grove, London N5 2AG
Tel: 020 7226 5375 Fax: 020 7704 0313
Email: admin@cdf.org.uk Website: www.cdf.org.uk

CDF has been working in this field for about 30 years and seeks to 'strengthen communities by ensuring the effective participation of people in determining the conditions which affect their lives through:

- providing support for community initiatives
- promoting best practice
- informing policy-makers at local and national level.'

CDF works directly with communities and also runs training programmes, conferences and an information service. It has also produced a wide range of publications.

Community Environment Resource Unit (CERU)
Set up by CDF with Government support to support and advise local and community-based organisations wishing to work on environmental issues. An office is being set up at the Burnley Community Enterprise Centre – Tel: 01282 47 3926.

Community Links
Canning Town Public Hall, 105 Barking Road, London E16 4HQ Tel: 020 7473 2270 Fax: 020 7473 6671
Email: community-links@geo2.poptel.org.uk

A social action centre based in east London and Sheffield. As well as working on community projects, each year it produces the Ideas Annual.

Community Matters
8–9 Upper St., London N1 OPQ
Tel: 020 7226 0189 Fax: 020 7354 9570
Email: communitymatters@communitymatters.org.uk
Website: www.communitymatters.org.uk

Works to expand the support provided to community organisations and represents their interests locally and nationally. It provides advice and training, partly through a community consultancy service, and runs a large annual conference.

Development Trusts Association (DTA)
20 Conduit Place, London W2 1HZ
Tel: 020 7706 4951 Fax: 020 7706 8447
Email: info@dta.org.uk Website: www.dta.org.uk

DTA links members of the growing network of development trusts in England, Wales and Northern Ireland. It advises on the development of new trusts and provides information and support, while also acting as an advocate on behalf of development trusts locally, nationally, and within Europe.

Inter-Action Trust
HMS President (1918), Nr Blackfriars Bridge, Victoria Embankment, London EC4Y OHJ
Tel: 020 7583 2652 Fax: 020 7583 2840
Email: chriscooper@inter-action.org.uk
Website: www.interaction.org.uk

Inter-Action encourages social and community enterprise projects and offers training and consultancy services to the voluntary and statutory sectors.

Neighbourhood Initiatives Foundation
(see Built environment)

Standing Committee on Community Development (SCCD)
356 Glossop Road, Sheffield S10 2HW
Tel: 0114 270 1718 Fax: 0114 276 7496
Email: admin@sccd.solis.co.uk

SCCD links community development organisations across the UK to share expertise and work on policy issues.

Further information

Publications

There are many publications in this field. CDF (see Main organisations) has a full publications list and a comprehensive web-site.

Building Community Strengths – a resource book on capacity building Skinner S. CDF 1997
A comprehensive guide to the tools of community development.

Gaining Ground – support for community groups
CDF 1995 A short guide for any community group on getting better organised.

Ideas Annual This is produced every year by Community Links, and describes dozens of good local projects. Each year's annual is themed on a different subject area.

Monitoring and Evaluation of Community Development in Northern Ireland Voluntary Activity Unit/Scottish Community Development Centre 1996. One of the best pieces of work available on how to evaluate (with indicators) community action. Available from Voluntary Activity Unit, DHSS, Castle Buildings, Stormont, Belfast BT4 3PP Tel: 028 90520504.

Unleashing the Potential: bring residents to the centre of regeneration Taylor M. Joseph Rowntree Foundation 1995. One of the most comprehensive works by the Rowntree Foundation which shows the importance and value of involving community groups.

Effective public participation

Involving local people and communities in making decisions that affect their lives and where they live and work is at the core of work towards more sustainable communities. It makes sense for local councils, housing agencies and environmental projects to consult with local people – local people know the real issues and problems in an area and may well have ideas on how to deal with them. It also makes sense for local people to know why participation is happening, and to understand what may be expected of them.

> KEY LINKAGES:
> Other relevant sections of this guide are:
> Safer environments, Sustainable towns and cities, Sustainable livelihoods, and Community development

Involvement, participation and consultation

These words may sound the same but can mean very different things in practice. 'Consultation' usually involves asking people questions through surveys etc. and using their replies, while 'participation' means getting those people involved in a process. This might mean designing and running a consultation exercise as part of a longer process.

From consultation to participation

One way of seeing the difference between consultation and participation is to look at the 'ladder of participation' developed by an American, Sherry Arnstein, in 1969. She suggested the differences between processes were based on the level of control which the participants have in any process.

The ladder of participation

1	Citizen control	
2	Delegated power	Degree of citizen power
3	Partnership	
4	Placation	
5	Consultation	Degree of tokenism
6	Informing	
7	Therapy	Non-participation
8	Manipulation	

This shows how consultation is just one approach to participation. It can help groups to work out what kind of involvement is being proposed. But it can make things seem too simple and it is misleading to see the 'ladder' as more than a basic guide. Different groups in the community may be at different levels on the ladder (they may have better contacts with the local council, and thus have more influence), and processes change and develop over time. Many other researchers have modified this ladder to try and make it more relevant.

The benefits of participation

Effective participation can have many advantages. Research done for the Department of the Environment in 1994 suggests that, 'at its best, community involvement can enable:

- processes to be speeded up
- resources to be used more effectively
- product quality and feelings of local ownership to improve
- added value to emerge
- confidence and skills to increase for all; and
- conflicts to be more readily resolved.'

Participation means different things to different people

Participation takes place in many different ways:

- people may participate in meetings about a new community centre because they want to know that it will meet their needs
- people may participate in a planning inquiry because they want to stop a supermarket being built on fields near their home
- people may participate in a regeneration process because they hope that they'll end up with a better place to live.

In all forms of participation, there are things in common: there is some form of process (meetings, surveys, special events etc.), which is usually set up by professionals (planners, architects, local council staff) with a view to getting the views and perhaps the involvement of the people who may be affected by the proposals. These processes can occur in different areas of society:

The one that affects most people is the UK planning system. Every city or district in the UK has a 'Development Plan' (these may be 'Structure Plans', 'Local Plans' or 'Unitary Development Plans'). The local council has to prepare a draft plan and to consult on it. This is 'statutory consultation': everyone has the right to object and to appear at a public enquiry. These processes are geared to professionals: local people appearing at an enquiry may find themselves cross-examined by barristers. Some local councils are now realising that this is not a good way to involve people and are trying to find better ways to link legal obligations with broader consultation.

The Government actively promotes participation in the guidance documents for bids to the Single Regeneration Budget (SRB) Challenge Fund. All bids to the Challenge Fund are meant to involve local communities and to show that partner organisations (including voluntary and community groups) 'have been fully involved in its preparation and will participate in its implementation if successful'. Any community group invited to get involved should be aware of its importance in the process, and should ensure that the bid includes programmes that will benefit it. Strategic Objective 7 for the Fund has, as a target, 'enhancing the capacity of local people to contribute to regeneration'. Some of the best examples of community involvement and participation can be found in regeneration programmes.

The NHS and Community Care Act charges each social services department with producing an annual Community Care Plan in active consultation with user groups and the public. Because health is a priority issue for so many people there are many good community development and health projects around the UK, most of which put a strong emphasis on participation and community development. This is reinforced at a city level by the growth of the 'Health for All' and 'Healthy Cities' programmes.

In 1992 the Rio Earth Summit called on local councils everywhere to 'consult with their communities' to develop their own 'Local Agenda 21' – an action plan for sustainable development in their area. The challenge of sustainable development is to link environmental issues with health, anti-poverty and economic development strategies. This requires participation processes that can link different organisations and audiences.

The politics of participation

Some people say that we all participate anyway, by voting for our representatives in local and national government. This 'representative democracy' is well established and open to all. However, many people have lost faith in politicians, or regard the day-to-day workings of local government as complicated and boring. As a result they choose not to vote, especially in local elections.

'Participative democracy' can certainly be more exciting and can get things done, but it is open to accusations of being undemocratic. This can happen in many ways: groups of two or three people can claim to represent a neighbourhood of thousands; tiny groups of political extremists can create groups with no real members, or a conservation group may decide to 'improve' a local park and create a wildlife area without consulting the children who play football there.

If participation is to flourish then it must work with and not against representative structures, and participation processes must be run in an open and democratic manner. Getting the balance between these two processes right is at the heart of effective governance.

Towards effective participation

Participation is an ongoing process. That process needs support not just at the time of the workshop or conference but in the months (and years) afterwards. Ongoing support can help counteract 'social exclusion' and can build a base for real long-term change. Support is needed for:

- personal development so that people have the confidence to become involved
- support and training to develop particular skills such as knowledge about design or financial management
- ensuring that information is made available to all people in appropriate form
- measures to monitor and ensure continued equal opportunities in terms of people participating at all stages.

Many participation or consultation processes fail to involve much of their potential audiences. It is easy to dismiss non-involvement as 'apathy', but there is plenty of evidence to show that where participation is done well, and there is a real chance of things changing, then people will be keen to have their say.

Ineffective participation processes are those which don't give people an adequate opportunity to talk, don't pay much attention to the ideas that come forward, and don't seem to change anything. People will feel they have given their time and energy for nothing. They may feel unhappy or angry and they are less likely to get involved in the future.

Participation fails for many reasons that include:

- a lack of adequate resourcing
- a failure to set up processes that genuinely encourage public involvement
- a lack of time
- a lack of trust in the process.

All these issues can be tackled. This can best be done by accepting that participative working requires commitment, resources and a clear policy. That policy should make it clear that the organisation in question is committed to public participation and will set standards for all community involvement work.

Many organisations can help improve participation

The UK Government requires local bodies such as heath trusts, regeneration agencies and councils to consult, yet sets no clear standards. If there is to be a real long-term improvement then there should be minimum standards for all statutory consultation, as there are in the planning process.

Many local councils take public participation very seriously, yet very few have clear policies. Any authority wishing to be seen to take this seriously could start by drawing up a draft policy and consult with its community on agreeing a final policy. Two central features of such a policy could be:

- all participation programmes should be adequately financed (for new developments we advocate a figure of 1% of the development cost as a guideline)
- all staff involved in community involvement should be adequately trained.

Annual reports from the council should include a 'review of participation', showing which major participative programmes it has run or supported, and how these were evaluated.

Companies and agencies involved in design, development or regeneration can also play an important role by promoting good practice in their work.

Community groups themselves can also play an important part in promoting better practice. Firstly they need to ensure that their own affairs are conducted in an open and participative manner and that all sectors of the community feel able to take part in their work. They can also play an important role by lobbying their local council and other agencies to ensure that they have policies and practices that will lead to more effective participation.

Tools and techniques for participation

Many special techniques for participation have been developed. These are all designed to make the process more effective by encouraging people to say what they really want and think.

Some techniques have names that describe them: 'Planning for Real', 'Parish Mapping', 'Round Tables', Focus Groups, Citizen Juries, Participatory Appraisal, Consensus Building, and so on; in other instances the process may just involve a series of well-run meetings over a few months, perhaps supported by newsletters, surveys and leaflets.

These techniques can be seen as tools that help people work together. It is always important that the right tool is used for each situation, and that the person running it knows how to use the tool properly.

The international dimension

The importance of participation was recognised by the governments of Europe when they agreed in 1998 the Arhus Convention on Freedom of Information, Public Participation and Access to Justice in Environmental Decision-Making. While this focuses mostly on national-level processes it recognises that standards should be set for work at all levels. This is likely to influence UK policy in these fields over the next few years.

Key organisations

Many organisations mentioned in other sections, notably community development and the built environment, are actively involved in promoting effective participation.

Centre for Community Visions – a New Economics Foundation project supporting innovative participation methods (see Main organisations)

Community Development Foundation (see Main organisations)

Tenants Participation Advisory Service (see Built environment)

Publications

The Shell Better Britain Campaign has a number of fact sheets on this work.

Building Democracy – community architecture in the inner cities. Graham Towers, UCL Press 1995. One of the best books on community involvement in the built environment.

Creating Involvement – a handbook of tools and techniques for effective community involvement. An excellent guide that is just what it says. Published by the Environment Trust. £15 from the Environment Trust, 150 Brick Lane, London E1 6RU.

Guidelines to the Community Involvement Aspect of the SRB Challenge Fund. CDF. This guide, updated for each SRB funding round, is to help staff and members of regeneration partnerships to plan for effective involvement.

Participation Works! Published 1998 by the New Economics Foundation, this identifies and describes 21 different participation techniques.

Community and Sustainable Development. Edited by Diane Warburton, Earthscan 1998. ISBN 1 85383 531 5. £14.95.

● Towards environmental justice

'No less than a decent environment for all: no more than a fair share of the earth's resources'
FoE Scotland campaign statement

The UK 'Blueprint for a Sustainable Community' is based on the idea of clear common standards, two of which are that every community should be able to enjoy a safe and healthy environment, and that every part of a community should be able to have its say.

Environmentalism in the UK has led to action on global pollution, endangered species, loss of rainforests and other high profile issues. But while these are crucial issues they have made little impact on poor or excluded communities. There has also been a tendency to suggest that the poor care less about the environment, or even that we should worry 'less about the poor, since they make less impact on the environment'.

Yet too often the poorest communities have the worst environments, such as badly-maintained 'sink' housing estates, and suffer disproportionately because of this. A poor local environment leads to health problems in many ways – hard-to-heat damp housing, air pollution or simply high levels of stress from an unsafe neighbourhood. There is also evidence that poorer communities get more than their share of polluting installations such as waste tips or incinerators. This has been described as 'environmental injustice'.

There is no reason to accept this situation. Sustainable communities will only be genuinely sustainable if every community is moving in the right direction. A society where some parts move towards sustainability at the expense of others is not a society which can claim to be sustainable.

Moves towards 'Environmental Justice' are developing in two areas:

- ensuring that everyone has access to justice
- development of an 'environmental justice' movement, as has happened in the USA.

KEY LINKAGES:
*Other relevant sections of this guide are:
The local environment and Strong communities*

Access to justice

There is no absolute legal right in the UK to a clean and safe environment, although the right to 'quiet enjoyment' of your home recognises that pollution may cut across that. While there are laws regulating the environment and directly or indirectly providing environmental rights, the process by which they can be used effectively is often not accessible and the rights of individuals and communities under those laws are not understood. This can mean that people may suffer environmental harm despite having legal means to solve the problem.

In 1998 the UK Government signed up to the Arhus Convention – the European Convention on Freedom of Information, Public Participation and Access to Justice in Environmental Decision-Making. At the time of writing it has not ratified this Convention but is expected to do so.

There are already organisations set up specifically to help people get access to justice on environmental issues. Such assistance can vary from single meetings to long-term involvement in a campaign, and may involve challenging polluters, negotiating on planning proposals, or providing advice to new environmental projects.

The environmental justice movement

'When we talk about environmental justice, we mean calling a halt to the poisoning and pollution of our poorer communities, from our rural areas to our inner cities'.

President Bill Clinton, June 1993

In the USA the disparities in the distribution of environmental hazards have led to the development of the 'environmental justice' movement. This network now links thousands of community-based organisations – most representing black, working-class or marginalised people and communities.

The environmental justice movement promotes the fair treatment of people of all races, income and culture with respect to the development, implementation and enforcement of environmental laws, regulations and policies. Fair treatment implies that no group of people should shoulder a disproportionate share of the negative environmental impact resulting from the execution of domestic and foreign policy programs.

The movement developed as evidence emerged that black communities suffer more environmental problems than white ones. A review of 64 major studies found clear environmental disparities either by race or income, with black communities suffering more than poor ones. From this work it emerged that:

- people of colour are twice as likely as white people to live in communities with a commercial hazardous waste management facility, and three times as likely to live in a community with multiple facilities or one of the largest hazardous waste landfills in the country
- higher levels of ambient pollution were correlated with lower incomes, and were higher for non-whites at all income levels
- non-white people die from acute exposure to hazardous substances at a rate more than 50% higher than that for whites. Cancer and many other diseases are correlated geographically with concentrations of industrial activity.

These figures have been challenged on various grounds: that they result from historical situations or that low-paid workers move to areas where there may be jobs. These challenges have in turn been refuted and research continues.

In October 1991 the first 'People of Colour Environmental Leadership Summit' brought together 650 African Americans, Latino Americans, Asian Americans and Native Americans and set out their 'Principles of Environmental Justice'. In 1992 the US Environmental Protection Agency responded and created an Office of Environmental Justice and set out 'Executive Order 12898, Federal Actions To Address Environmental Justice in Minority Populations and Low-Income

Populations'. This was signed into law by President Clinton on February 11 1994.

> *'The Order is important because it is a concrete sign that the administration has heard what many activists have been saying all along: environmental justice must become a priority at the highest levels of government.'*
>
> **Prof. Robert D. Bullard**,
> one of the organisers of the First National
> People of Color Environmental Summit

Environmental justice now brings together all ethnic minority, immigrant and native American groups throughout the USA, from Louisiana's 'Cancer Alley' to South Central Los Angeles, and from Native American reservations to Brooklyn and Chicago's South Side. It has led many traditional environmental organisations to set up programmes in this field, notably the National Wildlife Federation and Earth Island Institute's Urban Habitat Programme. In addition there are new radical environmental organisations, such as Communities Organised for a Better Environment, who are working to unite whole communities in areas that in the past have seen little or no environmental activity. These developments are challenging the 'environmental establishment' but are strengthening the broader environmental movement, both in the USA and across the world.

Action in the UK

Some suggest that such problems are not so prevalent in the UK. Certainly it is true that there are few communities where black ethnic groups form the majority of the population, and these are neighbourhoods rather than towns. However, while race and environmental links may not be so clear, the evidence of links between poverty and a bad environment is everywhere. Some of this may be historical circumstance, but that is no excuse for current planning decisions, where those decisions serve to reinforce current patterns of ill-health and deprivation.

The rapid development of GIS (geographical information systems) is now showing just how extensive the problem is. Work done by Friends of the Earth on mapping pollution and income levels shows clear correlations in many parts of the UK. Other organisations working on environmental epidemiology (researching how poor environments lead to health problems) also show clear links between environment and poverty. Friends of the Earth Scotland runs a major Campaign for Environmental Justice and works directly with communities who suffer the worst effects of pollution. Local authorities have also done work in this field: one example is the second 'Green Audit' by Lancashire County Council which provides a great deal of information about poverty and pollution issues mapped at a ward level.

Involving black and excluded communities

Excluded groups frequently lack the resources, time and capacity to mount effective local campaigns. This can make it easy for developers or councils to impose new problem developments on areas that already have more than their fair share. Thus, if there is a genuine desire to solve environment problems, and not merely shuffle them from one area to another, than 'levelling the playing field' must be a priority.

This means capacity-building in poorer communities, so that they can identify problems and threats, ideally well in advance, and take action against them. Environmental justice requires broader stakeholder participation in decision making, and this will be an issue for businesses, NGOs and local government.

Black organisations are now responding to this challenge. The 1990 Trust (see below) – the largest network of black organisations – has a sustainable development advisor. A few local authorities are developing specific programmes within their Local Agenda 21 work – much more could be done by local government in this area.

NGOs working on environment, regeneration or sustainable development should be actively seeking to develop partnerships with black or excluded communities. Some NGOs are developing work in this field: ELF (see below) has an outreach project targeted at excluded communities and is working with the 1990 Trust and the Environment Trust to provide information for the Black Environment Network.

If poorer communities are to take part in developing plans to improve their quality of life, they need an assurance that such work will indeed meet their needs. They must have an opportunity to express those needs, rather than merely being expected to work to an environmental agenda. The environmental justice movement provides examples and principles that show this approach works and works well.

Key organisations

Black Environment Network (BEN)
9 Llainwen Uchaf, Llanberis, Gwynedd Ll55 4LI
Tel/Fax: 01286 870715

BEN aims to promote the involvement of black and ethnic minority groups in environmental work. It has a number of projects around the UK.

EarthRights Solictors
Little Orchard, School Lane, Molehill Green, Takeley, Essex CM22 6PJ Tel/Fax: 07071 225011 or 01279 870391
Pager: 07669 127601 Email: earthrights@gn.apc.org
Website: www.gn.apc.org/earthrights

A solicitors' practice set up specially to take on environmental law cases. They have been involved in several important cases and can provide advice to campaigns and community groups.

The Environmental Law Foundation
Suite 309, 16 Baldwins Gardens, Hatton Square, London EC1N 7RJ Tel: 020 7404 1030
Fax: 020 7404 1032 Email: info@elf-net.org

ELF was set up to help people use the law to protect their environment. ELF works 'to ensure access to environmental justice for communities and individuals'. It provides access to specialists in environmental law and other environmental issues to individuals and community groups. Members of the public are given advice and can receive a free initial consultation with a local solicitor or technical expert. ELF also runs outreach services across the UK and in London to help raise awareness of people's environmental rights.

The Environment Trust
150 Brick Lane, London E1 6RU Tel: 020 7377 0481
Fax: 020 7247 0539 Email: info@envirotrust.org

The Environment Trust is working with the Bangladeshi community in Tower Hamlets on a range of environmental projects. The Trust also builds green homes and works on other projects.

Friends of the Earth Scotland
72 Newhaven Road, Edinburgh EH6 5QG Scotland, UK
Tel: 0131 554 9977 Fax: 0131 554 8656
Email: envjustice@foe-scotland.org.uk
Website: www.foe-scotland.org.uk

FoE Scotland has developed a strong campaign on environmental justice, working with both community groups and policy makers. It has an excellent introductory guide, *Protecting our Environment – a citizen's guide to environmental rights and action* (£4.95) and an excellent summary of its work on environmental justice.

Friends of the Earth (England, Wales & Northern Ireland) (see Main organisations)

Is also working in this field. It has produced *Factory Watch*, a computerised map of polluting installations across the country, and has now compared this data with socio-economic information, which is available on its website.

The 1990 Trust
Southbank Technopark, 90 London Road, London SE1 6LN Tel: 020 7717 1579 Fax: 020 7717 1585
Email: dondesilva@gn.apc.org
Website: www.blink.org.uk

The 1990 Trust is the foremost black network dealing with issues concerning the Asian, African and African-Caribbean communities across the UK. It has a newsletter and website and runs campaigns on many issues. It also has a Justice and Sustainability programme.

Further information

There is currently no single organisation in the UK that can provide a full referral service to black and ethnic minority groups nationally and around the UK. Anyone seeking to make links at a local level should contact their local Racial Equality Council. Nationally, the National Council for Voluntary Organisations (NCVO) has a Black Training and Enterprise Group that may be able to provide assistance (see Social sector organisations).

The most useful on-line service on environmental justice issues is available from the excellent US Environmental Justice website http://www.igc.org/envjustice. There are links from here to many related sites including government ones. A more detailed book on this subject is: *Unequal Protection Environmental Justice and Communities of Color*, edited by Robert D. Bullard ISBN: 0 87156 450 5.

● Access to information

'Public access to environmental information is a cornerstone for establishing adequate systems of public participation, and thus a basic instrument for ensuring effective environmental policy.'

Agenda 21, Chapter 40

'Environmental issues are best handled with the participation of all concerned citizens, at the relevant level. At the national level, each individual shall have appropriate access to information concerning the environment that is held by public authorities, including information on hazardous materials and activities in their communities, and the opportunity to participate in decision-making processes. States shall facilitate and encourage public awareness and participation by making information widely available'

Rio Declaration, UNCED 1992, p.11

IMPROVED ACCESS TO INFORMATION is important for fuller public involvement in environmental and social action issues. In turn, this will lead to better environments, healthier communities and a more sustainable way of living for all.

Information – the lifeblood of democracy

The European Union gives people rights of access to environmental information, and the UK has signed a new Europe-wide convention – the 'Aarhus Convention' on Access to Information, Public Participation in Environmental Decision-making and Access to Justice. The 'Aarhus Convention' has yet to be ratified but campaigning groups observe that, since the UK has signed up to its principles, national progress on putting these into practice should commence.

Initiatives such as 'right to know' campaigns and work on environmental justice (see that section) underpin the Aarhus Convention principles. Electronic access to environmental information is considered to be of vital importance, and for this reason the Aarhus Convention stipulates the need for environmental information to be compiled progressively in electronic format and made available to the public through telematic information networks.

Good practice includes:

- initiatives aiming to increase access to, and availability of, information that start to make sustainable development relevant to local people and encourage changes in work and lifestyles
- establishment of local environment centres to disseminate good practice messages, through education or training, or through 'hands-on' demonstration projects
- incorporating sustainable development considerations into professional training and education, for example, architects, designers and engineers.

Indicators for monitoring trends

Many authorities and organisations are now exploring the use of sustainability indicators as a means of helping to track progress and identify areas for action and the connections between them. Indicators have the potential to show whether we are achieving a better quality of life for everyone, but getting hold of the information needed to measure the chosen indicators can be a problem. Examples of headline and core indicators to be used to back UK Sustainable Development Strategy are available on DETR website.

Freedom of Information Bill 1999

The Government has now introduced this Bill, which ought to be the cornerstone of a more transparent society. At time of writing Government is under immense pressure to amend the Bill, which backtracks on many of the innovative ideas contained within a 1997 white paper. As it stands some proposals would actually reduce access to information. For example, information can be withheld if it is likely to be published at a later date, if it costs too much, and where new powers would let the Government allow exemptions as it chooses (even for a particularly embarrassing document).

The 'information explosion'

Electronic information advances in telecommunications technologies, especially through the development of the Internet, and the possibilities that these advances offer for processing, storing and transmitting information have opened many opportunities for different ways of working. For example, teleworking helps create livelihoods for people in remote areas, and the delivery of material electronically has helped individuals and groups that have physical limitations in reaching traditional storehouses of information.

For many Internet users, accessibility is more than just getting hold of a computer. Because people with hearing, sight and mobility disabilities often encounter enormous problems in using the web, the international body – the World Wide Web Consortium – is leading a drive to make the web more user-friendly for all types of users. Web designers and users can find guidelines and techniques for making sites more accessible on the Web Accessibility Initiative (WAI) site, www.w3.org/WAI.

Electronic access to information through web pages has proven to be a highly successful system and has certainly cut the number of requests for environmental information, which can now be satisfied in a more economical, efficient and faster way. The greater the environmental information made available to the public by these means, the better the accessibility of public information.

Further information

Government information, policy papers, consultation documents and information on legislative developments is available via the **Department of the Environment, Transport and the Regions** (DETR): DETR Free Literature, PO Box 236, Wetherby, S3 7NB Tel: 0870 1226 236 Fax: 0870 1226 237 or electronically – www.detr.gov.uk and www.open.gov.uk

In May 1999, the **Environment Agency** published a new pollution inventory – see www.environment-agency.gov.uk – which details releases of a core list of chemicals from the UK's largest industries (those regulated under Integrated Pollution Control). This is a welcome improvement on the old 'Chemical Releases Inventory' published on an occasional basis. But significantly, and for the first time, the Agency has published the data in a way that allows people to see which factories are in their area and what chemicals they are releasing.

Environmental Law Foundation's (see Environmental Justice) 'Access to Environmental Justice' project aims to ensure that all members of the community have access to information and advice about their environmental rights. The project will work with those who may suffer disproportionately from a poor environment, including those on low incomes, ethnic minority communities and people with disabilities. Publications and information produced as part of the campaign will be translated into six languages – Hindi, Bengali, Gujarati, French, Arabic, and Cantonese and, it is hoped, into Braille.

Right to know campaigns include **Friends of the Earth**'s Factory Watch, an Internet-based guide to UK factories that produce the most serious pollution. The interactive site uses official pollution data from the Environment Agency to provide information about pollution and health risks from 440 chemicals, emitted to ground, air and water by over 1,500 factories. It allows users to identify polluters releasing confirmed or suspected carcinogens in their local area. Data is retrieved by location, company or pollutant using postal codes. Website: www.foe.co.uk/factory-watch/intros/news.html

Case studies of good practice on Local Agenda 21 include work from the Local Agenda 21 Case Study Project whose steering committee selects case studies projects as examples of interesting (and not necessarily 'good') practice and to give some background on work in progress. Packs are available from **IDeA** (see Main organisations) or consult the Internet site at www.la21-uk.org.uk.

Information signposting services based with national organisations supplying information to stimulate local information include **Shell Better Britain Campaign** and **Going for Green**. (See Main organisations.)

Part Two

The organisations

The first section has listed over 120 organisations of all types and sizes that are working on sustainable development. These organisations can be grouped together in 'sectors' and one of the key themes in Agenda 21 is that each sector has a key role to play in working towards sustainable development.

This section looks at a range of key sectors and the organisations in those sectors that can provide information, advice and support.

The Government

GOVERNMENTS ARE CENTRAL TO ACHIEVING SUSTAINABLE DEVELOPMENT. International and inter-governmental agreements have set this process moving. National legislation and guidance create a framework for change, both nationally and locally. Without such a national framework, local efforts may find success impossible.

The UK Government's main objectives for sustainable development are:

- social progress which recognises the needs of everyone
- effective protection of the environment
- prudent use of natural resources and
- maintenance of high and stable levels of economic growth and employment.

The Department of the Environment, Transport and the Regions (DETR) is the government department which takes the lead in promoting sustainable development; its overarching aim being 'to improve the quality of life by promoting **sustainable development** at home and abroad, fostering economic prosperity and supporting local democracy'.

Committees

Government work on sustainable development involves:

- **The Cabinet Ministerial Committee on the Environment (ENV)**, chaired by the Deputy Prime Minister, is the principal decision-making body for Government policy on sustainable development and environmental protection.

- **The Green Ministers Committee**, chaired by the Minister for the Environment, reports to ENV. Ministers share best practice and are in charge of a programme to deliver sustainable development across Government. The Committee published the first in a series of annual reports in summer 1999.

- **The Environmental Audit Committee (EAC)** was set up in November 1997 by Parliament to consider the extent to which the policies and programmes of Government departments contribute to sustainable development and environmental protection. To date, the EAC has produced reports on Climate Change, Greening Government, the Multilateral Agreement on Investment, the Pre-Budget and the Comprehensive Spending Review.

Advisory bodies

The Government's work on sustainable development has been informed by:

- **The British Government Panel on Sustainable Development**: a high-level group appointed in 1994 by the then Prime Minister to advise the Government on sustainable development issues. It is chaired by Sir Crispin Tickell. In its 5th Report, published in February 1999, the Panel made recommendations on four major diverse topics: sustainable development and employment; environmental issues and the European Union; land legislation governing National Parks and Green Belts; and community and indigenous peoples' intellectual property rights over biological resources.

- **The UK Round Table on Sustainable Development**: a multi-stakeholder forum to help build consensus between people who have different viewpoints and perspectives about how to achieve the Government's vision of sustainable development. The Round Table is chaired by Derek Osborn, with the Deputy Prime Minister acting as President. There have been recent Round Table reports on agriculture and rural economy; approaches to sustainable business; monitoring and reporting; and devolved and regional dimensions of sustainable development.

These two bodies will, from 2000, merge and become **The Sustainable Development Commission**. The remit and working methods of this body are being discussed.

Other advisory bodies include:

- **The Advisory Committee on Business and the Environment (ACBE)** provides an avenue for dialogue between Government and business on environmental issues. Its membership includes top business and industry leaders.

- **The Sustainable Development Education Panel**: made up of members of business, local government, education and voluntary sectors, the panel was set up in 1998, and reports to the Deputy Prime Minister and the Secretary of State for Education and Employment. Its remit is to identify gaps and opportunities in education for sustainable development, highlight good practice, and to establish partnerships to get the sustainable development message across.

- **The Royal Commission on Environmental Pollution** is an advisory body, appointed by HM the Queen on the advice of the Prime Minister, and is independent of Government departments. The Commission does not confine itself to narrowly defined pollution issues, and analyses topics within the framework of sustainable development. The Royal Commission provides advice primarily in the form of reports on major studies it has carried out.

DETR oversees the work of a number of 'non-departmental public bodies' which carry out functions and provide specialist advice. These include the Environment Agency, and English Nature.

The National Sustainable Development Strategy

Following the Rio Earth Summit, the UK was one of the first countries in the world to prepare a national sustainable development strategy, published in 1994. A Government consultation process to revise this initial Strategy was held in Spring 1998, with the publication of the main consultation paper 'Opportunities for Change', and a series of consultation papers on Tourism, Business, Construction, Biodiversity, Forestry and Chemicals. Over 5,000 responses were received.

The strategy, *A Better Quality of Life* was published in May 1999. This document includes sections on:

- a sustainable economy
- managing the environment and resources
- international co-operation and development, and, significantly for this guide
- building sustainable communities

The section on sustainable communities makes closer links than any previous government document between poverty, health and environmental issues. While the strategy has few clear targets, it provides a very important overview to government thinking. It also sets out a set of national sustainable development indicators. A folder of summary documents is available on the internet or free of charge (see below).

Regional sustainable development

Government Offices for the Regions are staffed by the DETR, the Department of Trade and Industry, and the Department for Education and Employment. They handle local programmes and work with other regional interests to pursue sustainable development. A number of regions now have 'roundtables' involving a range of partners. Several are working on regional sustainable development strategies. Regional Development Agencies (RDAs) come into operation in April 1999 to provide co-ordinated economic development in the English regions. RDAs are required, as one of their five statutory purposes, to contribute to the achievement of sustainable development.

Local sustainable development

In 1998 central and local government published guidance for local authorities on why and how to produce an effective Local Agenda 21 strategy to meet the Prime Minister's target that all UK local authorities should have such a strategy in place by 2000. The Government supports local action for sustainability through modest funding for local initiatives and the LA21 case study project, and regional activities set up by the Government Offices in partnership with local government.

The Environmental Action Fund (EAF) provides £4m of central government support per year for English voluntary groups which advance the Government's sustainable development policies. The Fund also offers advice to groups on how to apply for grants, best practice, and other sources of support and advice.

Promotion

Going for Green (GfG), an initiative to promote lifestyle changes needed for sustainable development, was launched in 1995 and is supported by the Government. GfG activities include local and national publicity and events promoting a simple five-point Green Code focused around 'theme months'. The initiative supports a number of local sustainable communities projects.

'Doing your Bit' is a national publicity campaign run by DETR. Messages to the public are being integrated under the 'Are You Doing Your Bit' campaign, which communicates simple facts about lifestyles and the environment. The Children's Parliament on the Environment is a national writing and debating competition with regional and national finals to encourage children to do their bit for the environment.

Greening Government

'Greening Government' means integrating environmental considerations into decision-making at all levels across Government – policy as well as operations. *Guidance on Policy Appraisal and the Environment* was circulated in April 1998. *Implementing Environmental Management Systems in Government – guidelines for environmental managers and other key people* was launched in November 1998. Further guidance on better appraisal techniques is being developed.

The *Model Framework for Greening Government Operations* comprises a policy statement and a detailed improvement programme which UK Government departments can use to improve their environmental performance in estate management and other operational areas. It is supplemented by publications on green procurement, including a *Green Guide for Suppliers*, *Green Guide for Buyers* and *Choosing Environmentally Preferable IT Equipment*.

Other areas of work

Many other Government initiatives will affect progress towards sustainable development. Health Action Zones, 'New Deal' programmes for the Unemployed, for Schools, the Disabled, and Lone Parents will all affect communities across the UK, and are expecting participation to some degree by local people. Perhaps most significant is the New Deal for Communities, the National Strategy for Neighbourhood Renewal, which seeks to radically improve some of the worst areas to live in the UK. How far these plans will really incorporate and implement sustainable development principles is likely to be up to activity on the ground.

Large amounts of government money are also spent through the Single Regeneration Budget (SRB) programme. The sixth round of this major programme is in progress at time of going to print. The SRB guidelines have progressively developed and stressed the involvement of communities in these programmes.

The Government is also responsible for the National Lottery. The New Opportunities Fund for the Lottery distributes grants for health, education and environment initiatives. The first environment initiative within this fund is on 'Green Spaces and Sustainable Communities', which will be launched at the end of 1999.

Key organisations

Department of the Environment, Transport and the Regions (DETR)
Ashdown House, Victoria Street, London SW1E 6DE
Tel: (general enquiries): 020 7890 3000
Website: www.environment.detr.gov.uk (this is a very comprehensive website, with many documents available in full). The DETR also distributes much free material through DETR Free Literature, P.O. Box 236, Wetherby, W. Yorks. Tel: 0870 1226 236 Fax: 0870 1226 237.

- **Sustainable Development Unit** Tel: 020 7890 6468
- **Environmental Action Fund** Tel: 020 7890 7038
- **Secretariat for Round Table** and **Panel on Sustainable Development** Tel: 020 7890 4964 (Panel Website: http://www.open.gov.uk/panel-sd/homesd.htm)
- **Secretariat for Panel on Sustainable Development Education** Tel: 020 7890 6693
- **Secretariat for Advisory Committee on Business and the Environment** Tel: 020 7890 6494
- **The Royal Commission on Environmental Pollution** Website: http://www.rcep.org.uk
- **'Doing Your Bit'** campaign office Tel: 0171 544 3131 Website: www.doingyourbit.org.uk

Environment Agency
Rio House, Waterside Drive, Aztec West, Bristol BS32 4UD (general enquiries) Tel: 0645 333111
Website: www.environment-agency.gov.uk

The Environment Agency was set up in 1995 and is responsible for integrated management of air, land, and water within the UK environment, through education, prevention and enforcement. It is the chief Government body for pollution regulation and control, waste management, river quality and much more.

Going for Green
Elizabeth House, The Pier, Wigan WN3 4EX
Tel: 01942 612621 Website: www.gfg.iclnet.co.uk

Going for Green is a Government-funded awareness campaign on environmental issues and sustainable development. It promotes individual and community activity, and is in late 1999 launching a major 'sustainable communities' campaign.

Publications

A Better Quality of Life – a strategy for sustainable development for the United Kingdom, DETR (1999) £11.80 from The Stationery Office Bookshops.

Guidance on Enhancing Public Participation, DETR (1998)

Planning for Sustainable Development: Towards Better Practice, DETR (1998)

Sustainable Regeneration Good Practice Guide, DETR (1998)

The Environment Agency and Going for Green produce quarterly free newsletters.

● Local government

LOCAL GOVERNMENT, AS THE MOST LOCAL LEVEL OF GOVERNMENT, has a central role to play in building sustainable communities. Much of this work is being led by Local Agenda 21 programmes but many other local government activities are also important.

Local Agenda 21

Chapter 28 of Agenda 21 calls on all councils to work with their communities to draw up and implement local plans (Local Agenda 21s) for sustainable development and 'to enter into a dialogue with its citizens, local organisations and private enterprises.' Through consultation and consensus building, local authorities will 'learn from citizens and from local, civic, community, business and industrial organisations and acquire the information needed for formulating the best strategies'.

Local government associations in the UK have actively promoted this idea and set up the UK Local Agenda 21 initiative to promote the concept, with a cross-sectoral steering group to oversee the process and to produce guidance.

Local authorities were already engaged in a wide range of environmental initiatives, ranging from recycling to nature conservation, but Agenda 21 introduced the concept of sustainable development, encouraging them to think about ways of integrating environmental issues with social and economic issues. This holistic approach has appealed to many authorities as it is relevant to virtually every aspect of their work, from anti-poverty measures to planning. It also encouraged them to think in terms of win/win solutions, such as energy conservation measures not only reducing CO2 emissions, but also making homes warmer and healthier for those on low incomes. Councils also have a key role in building awareness of sustainable development issues, in ensuring that local concerns and aspirations are fully taken into account when drawing up plans, and in leading and encouraging activity.

There is no legal obligation on local authorities to engage in a Local Agenda 21 (LA21) process, but the Government has encouraged local authorities to do so, with Tony Blair calling on all local authorities to draw up Local Agenda 21 plans by 2000. Over 80% have committed themselves to doing so.

Much material is now available to guide local authorities on the development of their Local Agenda 21 and other work on sustainable development. This is available from the Sustainable Development Unit within the local government Improvement and Development Agency (IDeA, formerly the Local Government Management Board). Material includes guidance notes on specific topics such as food, water, involving young people, ethnic minorities and so on, to guidance on process issues such as using consensus building techniques and how to undertake sustainability reporting.

Information is also available on the European Eco-Management and Audit Scheme (EMAS). The Sustainable Development Unit also services a network of local authority officers who are working on local sustainability issues, providing them with advice, organising training, seminars and conferences.

The wider local government agenda

The Local Government Association (LGA) is the main representative body, and all English and Welsh authorities are members of the LGA which lobbies on their behalf and represents their interest in discussions with Government and others. The LGA's policy and lobbying work covers every area of local government activity and it works in partnership with the IDeA to promote LA21 and sustainable development.

The LGA has a number of relevant policy programmes, including several that respond to the Government's new agenda of 'Modernising Local Government'. This includes proposals on Best Value, democracy, and a new form of 'community planning' which seeks to improve the environmental, economic and social wellbeing of an area. This will clearly need to link with work on LA21, which has the same remit.

Best Value is a new process, to come into effect from April 2000, which aims to secure 'continuous improvement' in all local authority functions and seeks to combine 'economy, efficiency, and effectiveness'. While there is no direct mention of environmental quality or sustainability, there is a duty on councils to consult extensively about service delivery, and to make detailed plans for this work. Key areas will include transport, housing, and environmental services.

Other relevant local government work includes:

- the LGA Democracy Network, which works to develop and improve local democracy and has done a lot of work on improving local participation
- a policy statement on 'Energy services for sustainable communities'
- involvement in the 'Don't Choke Britain' campaign on traffic reduction
- a review of research work on environmental taxation and implications for local government
- assessment of how Best Value programmes can promote sustainability
- guidance to local authority practitioners on sustainable economic regeneration.

Key organisations

Association of Local Authorities in Northern Ireland (ALANI) (see Main organisations)

Convention of Scottish Local Authorities (COSLA) (see Main organisations)

The Local Government Association (LGA)
26 Chapter Street, London SW1P 4ND
Tel: 020 7664 3000/3131 Fax: 020 7664 3030
Website: http://www.lga.gov.uk

This is the main representative body for local government in England and Wales. It covers all areas of concern to local government and has a wide range of publications and special interest networks.

The Improvement and Development Agency
76–86 Turnmill Street, London EC1M 5QU
Tel: 020 7296 6599 Fax: 020 7296 6666
Email: local.agenda.21@lgmb.gov.uk
Website: www.la21-uk.org.uk

The IDeA, formerly the Local Government Management Board, works with the LGA to provide support and advice for local government. It is working on integrating sustainable development into all aspects of local authority work, and is developing an on-line information resource. It will provide a support service to local councils working on LA21 until July 2000 and then will work on Best Practice and community planning. A publications list on LA21 is available from the Best Practice Unit and many of the free publications are accessible on the website, plus updates and other information of interest. The Unit also supports a publication produced by the University of Westminster – EG, *Local Environment News*. This monthly publication is aimed primarily at local authority officers, but is also of interest to a wider audience. Further information from: **Environment Resource and Information Centre (ERIC)** University of Westminster, 35 Marylebone Road, London, NW1 5LS Tel: 020 7911 5000 ext. 3136
Fax: 020 7911 5171 Email: walkerh@wmin.ac.uk
Website: www.wmin.ac.uk/eric

Social sector organisations

THE UK HAS A HUGE AND DIVERSE VOLUNTARY SECTOR. While few of the organisations listed below work directly on sustainable development, their work will certainly affect UK sustainability, and they may well be able to provide advice and assistance to relevant projects. Those listed are only a tiny part of the sector: the best guide is the NCVO Voluntary Agencies Directory, which is updated annually.

Some key organisations

Age Concern England
Astral House, 1268 London Road, London SW16 4ER
Tel: 020 8679 8000 Fax: 020 8679 6069
Website: www.ace.org.uk

A confederation of 1,400 national and local organisations which promote the well being of older people. They work for more positive attitudes towards older people and aging; influence and develop public policies that affect older people; and encourage effective care for old people and choice and opportunity. Issues of concern include fuel poverty, the rise in water prices, and transport.

Charter88
16–24 Underwood Street, London N1 7JQ
Tel: 020 7684 3888 Fax: 020 7684 3889
Website: www.charter88.org.uk

The independent campaign for a modern and fair democracy. Its goals are political institutions which are just, open and accountable, and a culture that encourages the participation of every citizen. It has run a Citizens Enquiry, looking at popular perceptions of democracy in the UK. Current campaign priorities include human rights, voting reform and democratic exclusion.

Child Poverty Action Group
94 White Lion Street, London N1 9PF
Tel: 020 7253 3406 Fax: 020 7490 0561

Promotes action for the relief of poverty. Activities include providing a national service of welfare benefits advice and training, legal test cases to ensure poor families receive the benefits due to them, researching family poverty in the UK and informing the public, MPs and the media.

Church Action on Poverty
Central Buildings, Oldham Street, Manchester M1 1JT
Tel: 0161 236 9321 Fax: 0161 237 5359

Aims to educate people especially in the churches about the causes and extent of poverty in Britain and to campaign for changes that assist the least well off. Works at local and national level to change public attitudes and policies to promote lasting solutions to the problem of poverty.

Community Service Volunteers
237 Pentonville Road, London N1 9NJ
Tel: 020 7278 6601 Fax: 020 7833 0149

CSV supports national programmes of community service, which include volunteering by young people and by retired people, CSV Education, media projects and CSV Environment (which is run from a Birmingham office Tel: 0121 322 2008). There is also a Scottish office which works on LA21 issues (see Scotland section).

Consumers Association
2 Marylebone Road London NW1 4DF
Tel: 020 7830 6000 Fax: 020 7830 6220
Website: www.which.net

An independent organisation which conducts research into goods and investigations into services and reports the results via *Which?*, *Holiday Which?*, *Gardening Which?* and *Which? Way to Health*. It represents consumer interests and campaigns for improvements in goods and services.

Federation of Independent Advice Centres
4 Dean's Court, St Paul's Churchyard, London EC4V 5AA Tel: 020 7489 1800 Fax: 020 7489 1804

Promotes the provision of independent advice services and supports centres delivering independent advice to the public. FIAC acts as a co-ordinating network and voice for centres, providing a discussion forum on issues of concern, and helps formulate and promote policies with regard to advice work.

Help the Aged
St James' Walk, Clerkenwell Green, London EC1R 0BE
Tel: 020 7253 0253 Fax: 020 7250 4474

Aims to improve the quality of life of older people, particularly those who are frail, isolated or poor. Develops practical aid programmes by identifying needs, raising public awareness and fundraising, with an emphasis on day centres and day hospitals, community alarms, research, sheltered housing and reminiscence work.

Law Centres Federation
Duchess House 18–19 Warren Street, London W1P 5DB
Tel: 020 7387 8570 Fax: 020 7387 8368

Encourages the development of publicly funded legal services for those most disadvantaged in society and promotes the 'law centre' model as the best means of achieving this. Radical changes to the way legal aid operates are underway, with alternative methods of funding legal help and refocusing legal aid to social welfare law. LCF argues that the definition of a community legal service should be broad, and it should provide legal education, community work, group casework and legal support to campaigns.

Low Pay Unit
27-29 Amwell Street, London EC1R 1UN
Tel: 020 7713 7616 Fax: 020 7713 7581

Investigates and publicises low pay, poverty and related issues. Lobbies Government and publishes reports and provides a rights service for the general public and their advisers.

MIND – the National Association for Mental Health
Granta House, 15 Broadway, London E15 4BQ
Tel: 020 8519 2122 Helpline: 020 8522 1728

MIND campaigns for good quality local mental health services, and has seven regional offices and around 200 local organisations.

Money Advice Association
Gresham House, 24 Holborn Viaduct, London EC1A 2BN Tel: 020 7236 3566 Fax: 020 7329 1579

Promotes the development of free, independent money advice services and works to improve policies affecting the financial interests of consumers. Co-ordinates training for agencies nationwide.

National Centre for Volunteering
Regent's Wharf, 8 All Saints Street London N1 9RL
Tel: 020 7520 8900 Fax: 020 7520 8910
Email: volunteering@thecentre.org.uk
Website: www.volunteering.org.uk

The centre works to promote all aspects of volunteering and co-ordinates UK Volunteers Week

National Consumer Council (NCC)
20 Grosvenor Gardens, London SW1W 0DH
Tel: 020 7730 3469 Fax: 020 7730 0191

The NCC promotes the interests of consumers of goods and services of all kinds, whether publicly or privately owned, paying particular attention to disadvantaged consumers. It applies tests including access, choice, information, redress, safety, fairness and representation. It is on the UK Round Table on Sustainable Development and publishes a range of publications on environmental issues.

National Association of Councils for Voluntary Service (NACVS)
3rd floor, Arundel Court, 177 Arundel Street, Sheffield S1 2NU Tel: 0114 278 6636
Email: nacvs@nacvs.org.uk Website: www.nacvs.org.uk

NACVS is a large network that has extensive information on local groups.

National Association of Volunteer Bureaux
St Peters College, College Road, Saltley, Birmingham B8 3TE Tel: 0121 327 0265 Fax: 0121 327 3696

Provides information about local volunteer bureaux, as well as training and support for the bureaux.

National Association of Citizens Advice Bureaux
Myddelton House, 115–123 Pentonville Road, London N1 9LZ Tel: 020 7833 2181
Website: www.nacab.org.uk

The Citizens Advice Bureaux Service handles over six million problems a year. Much of its work is poverty-related, such as social security benefits, debt, housing and employment. There are 700 bureaux with another 1,400 outreach services e.g. in hospitals and magistrates courts. A new website project will make more information available direct to the public.

National Council for Voluntary Organisations (NCVO)
Regent's Wharf, 8 All Saints Street, London N1 9RL
Tel: 020 7713 6161 Fax: 020 7713 6300
Website: www.ncvo-vol.org.uk

Champions the cause of the voluntary sector in England, working with government, business and the public sector. NCVO runs a free Voluntary Sector Helpdesk (0845 600 4500) answering queries about the voluntary sector, and a trustee helpline. Its priorities are funding for the sector, improving the regulatory framework, trustee development, advice development and European work. It supports its members in the use of IT, including discounted software, and runs an Urban Forum.

RADAR – Royal Association for Disability and Rehabilitation
12 City Forum, 250 City Road, London EC1V 8AF
Tel: 020 7250 3222 Fax: 020 7250 0212
Website: www.radar.org.uk

RADAR works on every aspect of disability as a pressure group, and advises on access, mobility, holidays, housing, employment and education.

● Environment and development non-governmental organisations (NGOs)

THIS SECTION COVERS NON-GOVERNMENTAL ORGANISATIONS whose work raises awareness and supports sustainability initiatives at both the national and local level. Sustainable development is leading to closer links between traditional environmental networks, the social development sector and the world development movement and this is reflected in these groups' published literature and campaigning activities.

Black Environment Network (BEN)
(see Towards environmental justice)

British Trust for Conservation Volunteers (BTCV)
36 St Mary's Street, Wallingford, Oxon OX10 0EU
Tel: 01491 839766 Fax: 01491 839646
Email: information@btcv.org.uk
Website: www.btcv.org.uk

BTCV is the UK's leading practical conservation charity with 90 offices throughout England, Wales and Northern Ireland. BTCV's Group Membership scheme offers advice as well as competitive rates on tools, insurance and protective clothing. BTCV also runs working holidays.

Christian Aid
PO Box 100. London SE1 7RT Tel: 020 7620 4444
Website: www.christian-aid.org.uk

Christian Aid is one of the largest development charities, and works on all aspects of global development as well as running education and anti-poverty programmes.

Communities Against Toxics (CATs)
PO Box 29, Ellesmere Port, CH66 3TX
Tel/Fax: 0151 339 5473
Email: ralph@tcpublications.freeserve.co.uk

CATs is a strong grassroots network of about 80 groups throughout the UK working on issues such as toxic waste, landfills, and water pollution.

Council for the Protection of Rural England (CPRE)
Warwick House, 25 Buckingham Palace Road,
London SW1W 0PP
Tel: 020 7976 6433 Fax: 020 7976 6373
Email: info@cpre.org.uk
Website: www.greenchannel.com/cpre

The CPRE campaigns, lobbies and researches on all aspects of the rural environment, including issues such as housing, energy and transport.

Ethical Consumer Research Association (ECRA)
Unit 21, 41 Old Birley Street, Manchester M15 5RF
Tel: 0161 226 2929 Fax: 0161 226 6377
Email: ethicon@mcr1.poptel.org.uk

Publishers of 'Ethical Consumer' magazine, ECRA promotes universal human rights, environmental sustainability and animal welfare by encouraging a wider understanding of the ability of ethical purchasing to address these issues.

Environment Council
212 High Holborn, London WC1V 7VW
Tel: 020 7836 2626 Fax: 020 7242 1180
Email: info@envcouncil.org.uk
Website: www.greenchannel.com/tec

This independent charity raises awareness of 'stakeholder dialogue' and runs a number of environmental programmes, including Conservers at Work, assisting business with environmental matters, including mediation work.

Forum for the Future
9 Imperial Square, Cheltenham, Gloucestershire
GL50 1QB Tel: 01242 26299
Website: www.forumforthefuture.org.uk

The Forum works to build a sustainable way of life through a positive, solutions-oriented approach. It runs a number of programmes with businesses and local authorities, including the Natural Step initiative, and has a sustainable local economy project. It also publishes 'Green Futures' magazine.

Friends of the Earth England Wales and Northern Ireland (see Main organisations)

FOE Scotland (see Towards environmental justice)

Global Action Plan (GAP)
8 Fulwood Place, London WC1V 6HG
Tel: 020 7405 5633 Fax: 020 7831 6244
Email: all@gapuk.demon.co.uk

GAP encourages people to take practical environmental action in their homes, workplaces, schools and communities through a series of programmes.

Going for Green (see Main organisations)

Green Alliance
40 Buckingham Palace Road, London SW1W 0RE
Tel: 020 7233 7433 Fax: 020 7233 9033
Email: ga@greenalliance.demon.co.uk
Website: www.greenalliance.demon.co.uk

The Green Alliance works to promote environmental and sustainability issues within Government through seminars, research and publications. Membership is by invitation.

Greenpeace
Canonbury Villas, London N1 2PN
Tel: 020 7354 5100 Fax: 020 7359 4062.

Greenpeace is the largest international campaigning group working to protect the natural environment. As well as high-profile actions it carries out research, produces briefings and seeks to involve supporters in lobbying.

Groundwork Foundation (see Main organisations)

International Society for Ecology and Culture (ISEC)
Apple Barn, Reek, Dartington TQ9 6GP
Tel: 01803 86 8650

ISEC works through campaigns, videos, books and study/action groups to raise awareness about the social and environmental impact of development and economic globalisation, in north and south; and promotes sustainable alternatives at community and policy level.

Learning Through Landscapes (LTL)
Southside Offices, The Law Courts, Winchester SO23 9DL Tel: 01962 846258 Fax: 01962 869099 Email: charity@tcp.co.uk

LTL runs innovative programmes encouraging better use of school grounds for education about sustainable development.

National Society for Clean Air and Environmental Protection (NSCA)
136 North Street, Brighton BN1 1RG
Tel: 01273 326313 Email: admin@nsca.org.uk
Website: www3.mistral.co.uk/cleanair

The NSCA works to secure environmental improvement by promoting the reduction of air pollution, noise and other contaminants through lobbying, training, advice and research.

New Economics Foundation
(see Main organisations)

Oxfam (see Main organisations)

Projects in Partnership (PiP)
2nd floor, The Tea Warehouse, 10a Lant Street, London SE1 1QR Tel: 020 7407 8585
Fax: 020 7407 9555

PiP promotes sustainable development, specialising in creating solutions through participation and partnership.

RSNC, The Wildlife Trusts
The Kiln, Waterside, Mather Road, Newark NG24 1WT
Tel: 01636 677711 Fax: 01636 670001
Email: info@wildlife-trusts.cix.co.uk
Website: www.wildlifetrust.org.uk

The Wildlife Trust's national office links and supports the many county-level WildlifeTrusts throughout the UK. It has also been running the 'Environment City' project in six cities.

Save the Children Fund
17 Grove Lane, London SE5 8RD Tel: 020 7703 5400
Website: www.oneworld.org/scf

Save the Children works in 50 countries including the UK. It aims for sustainable solutions to problems affecting children, supporting them, their families and communities to be self-sufficient by providing emergency relief alongside long-term development and prevention work. Work in the UK includes mobile toy libraries, children's clubs and transport to playgroups in isolated rural areas. It promotes better mental health by listening to young people's views.

SERA
11 Goodwin Street, London N4 3HQ
Tel: 020 7263 7389 Fax: 020 7263 7424
Email: seraoffice@aol.com
Website: www.users.aol.com/seraoffice

SERA is the Labour Environment Campaign and works to promote environmental issues within the Labour movement.

Shell Better Britain Campaign
(see Main organisations)

Soil Association (see Food)

Tidy Britain Group
Elizabeth House, Wigan Pier, Wigan WN3 4EX
Tel: 01942 824620 Fax: 01942 824778
Email: enquiries@tidybritain.org.uk
Website: www.tidybritain.org.uk

A charity concerned with environmental improvements and the eradication of litter. It promotes local, regional and national programmes, including Eco-schools, Britain in Bloom, Tidy Britain Awards, National Spring Clean, and Blue Flag Seaside Awards. It has a close relationship with Going for Green.

Town and Country Planning Association (TCPA)
(see Built environment)

UNED–UK (see Main organisations)

World Development Movement (WDM)
25 Beehive Place, London SW9 7QR
Tel: 020 7737 6215 Fax: 020 7274 8232
Website: www.wdm.org.uk

WDM works to raise awareness and promote action about the gross inequalities and poverty issues affecting many people, especially in developing countries. Calls for a re-direction of spending away from the military and helps to promote Fair Trade issues.

World Wide Fund for Nature (WWF-UK)
(see Main organisations)

● Community sector organisations

COMMUNITY SECTOR ORGANISATIONS do not generally have sustainability as a prime aim and the very word may not be part of their language. But the work of many groups addresses issues related to sustainable development. Skills development, informal social education, and supporting and sustaining local communities are at the core of community work and sustainable development.

It has been suggested that more of the population learn and experience civic skills and build talent within community groups than from any other source. Such groups are drivers of community development initiatives, stimulating self-sufficiency within communities and providing for the varied needs of individuals, neighbours and groups within a locality. There are over

500,000 community sector groups in the UK – possibly more than one million. Quite literally, millions of people are involved at varying degrees of intensity with local organisations.

What is the community sector?

The community sector is a distinct part of the voluntary sector with its own needs and priorities. The UN recognises this distinction and defines larger, often policy-focused groups as NGOs (non-governmental organisations) and smaller groups, focused on a specific area or issue as CBOs (community-based organisations). Both sectors have important, but different, roles in civic life. Often they work productively together, but there are important differences.

Many traditional voluntary organisations were set up to provide services and as such are built on an ethos of charity. They are normally run by trustees and professionals for the benefit of others, who are often considerably different in terms of class, ethnicity and status. Such groups usually employ paid staff and while some are small, others are very large, extremely well-resourced and can have a national influence.

Community groups on the other hand are based on collective activity, where individuals and groups collaborate either for their own benefit, or for their families and neighbours, or for people who share similar concerns or a sense of common identity. The underlying aim is improving the overall quality of collective life and conditions. Community groups tend to be small, usually with no paid staff, and often play a representational/campaigning role as well as having mutual support and self-help functions. They are primarily accountable to their own members/users and secondly to the communities within which they operate.

This activity may be undertaken by groups acting within their own neighbourhood, or within a community of interest and/or identity. The key features are involvement around shared issues/interests with an ethos of mutuality and self-help, usually at a grass-roots level. It is a continuum which extends from informal networks and general 'neighbourly' activities, through informal community groups and campaigns, to formally constituted community-based organisations.

There are two main types of community group:

- groups based on a locality, usually a small local area
- groups based on a community of interest, for example, based on gender, race, or relating to a particular situation

Organisations based around a community of interest often have a geographical focus, which can be a much larger area or region. Examples include playgroups, voluntary youth groups, community associations, women's groups, voluntary sports and drama clubs, self-help groups, black and ethnic minority community groups, community refugee groups, village halls, tenants' and residents' groups, local action groups and amenity societies, community city farms, local disability action groups, and support groups.

The Community Sector Coalition

National organisations supporting community-based groups have formed the Community Sector Coalition. The basic aim is to increase recognition of, and support for, the community sector. Specifically, the Coalition aims to:

- promote greater awareness and understanding of the distinctive and diverse nature and needs of the community sector
- increase recognition of the value and contribution the community sector makes to civil society and the social economy
- identify the support needs of community sector groups and press for greater resourcing of them
- examine current social policy to help illustrate the distinctive nature and needs of the community sector and to highlight relevant implications.

Key organisations and networks

Most of these national networks have hundreds and, in some cases, thousands of local community sector organisations within their membership.

ACRE (Action with Communities in Rural England)
Somerford Court, Somerford Road, Cirencester, Glos GL7 1TW Tel: 01285 653477
Fax: 01285 654537 Email: acre@acre.org.uk
Website: www.acreciro.demon.co.uk

ACRE is the contact point for 38 county-based rural communities councils in England, and also runs the Village Halls Forum. It provides advice and information and has an extensive publications list.

British Association of Settlements and Social Action Centres (see Community development)

Centres for Change
43 St Giles, Oxford OX1 3LW Tel: 01865 316338
Fax: 01865 516288 Email: cfc@centres.demon.co.uk
Website: www.centres.demon.co.uk

A network of community buildings and resource centres working on environment, peace, sustainability and social justice issues.

Community Development Foundation (CDF)
(see Main organisations)

Community Matters (see Community development)

The Community Sector Coalition can be contacted via Email: csc@communitymatters.org.uk

Confederation of Indian Organisations (UK)
5 Westminster Bridge Road, London SE1 7XW
Tel: 020 7928 9889 Fax: 020 7620 4025
Email: cio@gn.apc.org.

CIO works with Asian organisations across the UK and can provide information and contacts with local organisations.

Development Trusts Association
(see Community development)

Federation of City Farms and Community Gardens (see Food)

Standing Conference for Community Development (see Community development)

Further information

All the above organisations produce newsletters, magazines and other literature, in some cases only for member organisations. Contact individual groups for publications lists. One publication which may be of special interest is **Community Matters' 'Environmental Action Pack'**, price £6.00 to non-members. This contains ideas and resources specifically designed for community groups working to improve the quality of their environment.

● Women's organisations

'Governments should take active steps to implement ... Measures to review policies and establish plans to increase the proportion of women involved as decision makers, planners, managers, scientists and technical advisers in the design, development and implementation of policies and programmes for sustainable development and also measures to strengthen and empower women's bureaux, women's non-governmental organizations and women's groups in enhancing capacity-building for sustainable development'

Agenda 21, Chapter 24

THE RIGHT OF WOMEN TO HAVE A VOICE in environmental decision-making is enshrined in the outcomes of the 1992 Earth Summit. Principle 21 of the Rio Declaration states that 'Women have a vital role in environmental management and development. Their full participation is therefore essential to achieving sustainable development.' This is true at all levels of society. As consumers and producers, caretakers of their families and educators, women play an important role in promoting sustainable development through their own concern for the quality and sustainability of life for present and future generations.

Despite the welcome words of Agenda 21, women's contribution to sustainable development remains largely unrecognised. Their unwaged work of providing shelter, food and water, healthcare, childcare and emotional support contributes incalculably to human well being. It explains why women – who are expected to do the work of creating, protecting and sustaining human life – are at the fore of international movements and local groups defending and protecting the environment.

According to the International Labour Organisation, women do 66% of the world's work for 5% of the income and 1% of the assets. Women's lack of resources, South and North, prevents them from making their potential contribution to sustainable development. They are rarely included in the process of formulating the policies which govern the day-to-day framework of their consumer choices, environmental management, and caring work. The poorer the woman, the harder she has to work to make up for destructive 'development', and the less likely she is to be included in any consultation.

Women are rarely trained as professional natural resource managers with policy-making capacities, such as land-use planners, agriculturalists, or environmental lawyers. Even where women have received such training, they are often under-represented in formal institutions with policy-making capacities and they are only rarely equal participants in the management of financial and corporate institutions whose decision-making most significantly affects environmental quality.

There are also institutional weaknesses in co-ordination between women's non-governmental organisations (NGOs) and national institutions dealing with environmental issues, despite the recent rapid growth and visibility of women's NGOs working on these issues at all levels. Women have often played leadership roles or taken the lead in promoting an environmental ethic, reducing resource use, and reusing and recycling resources to minimise waste and excessive consumption.

In addition, women's contributions to environmental management, including through grass-roots and youth campaigns to protect the environment, have often taken place at the local level, where decentralised action on environmental issues is most needed and decisive. Governments and other actors should actively and visibly promote a gender perspective in all policies and programmes, including, as appropriate, an analysis of the effects on women and men, respectively, before decisions are taken.

Key organisations

CHANGE
106 Hatton Square, 16–16a Baldwins Gardens, London EC1N 7RT Tel: 020 7430 0692
Email: change_clc@compuserve.com

CHANGE runs National and International campaigns on economics, poverty, employment and violence. They are involved in follow-up work on the Beijing Women's Conference.

Engender
c/o One Parent Families, 13 Gayfield Square, Edinburgh EH1 3NX Tel: 0131 558 9596
Fax: 0131 557 9650

Engender is an information, research and networking organisation for women in Scotland, working locally and internationally to improve women's lives and increase their power and influence. The organisation campaigns to ensure that women and their concerns have greater visibility and equal representation at all levels of Scottish society.

The Fawcett Society
5th Floor, Beech Street, London EC2Y 8AD
Tel: 020 7628 4441 Fax: 020 7628 2865

The Society campaigns for equality between men and women, especially in politics and employment. They are in the process of setting up local groups.

National Federation of Women's Institutes
104 New Kings Road, London SW6 4LY
Tel: 020 7371 9300 Fax: 020 7736 3652
Website: www.nfwi.org.uk

The WI is the largest voluntary women's organisation in the UK. The WI brings women together to enjoy friendship within their local communities and works to improve the quality of life in the community. They campaign on national and international social, environmental and consumer issues which concern women and their families, and provide lifelong learning opportunities for women to develop their skills, talents and sense of citizenship.

National Women's Network
83 Margaret Street, London W1N 7HB
Tel: 020 8809 2388

The Network facilitates contact between women concerned with international and feminist issues and promotes networking between women. They publish a newsletter, including events and publications, every two months.

Oxfam (see Main organisations)

United Nations Environment and Development – UK Committee (UNED–UK)
(see Main organisations)

UNED-UK has several gender-related projects. The Gender 21 Initiative co-ordinates projects developing the role of women in achieving sustainable development. To do this, the initiative organises seminars and briefings as well as producing reports and guidance notes. Other gender-related projects include: Gender and Tourism; Gender, Consumption and Production; Stakeholder Toolkit for women.

UNIFEM–UK
4A Hedgerly Close, Cambridge CB3 0EW
Tel: 01223 352 339 Fax: 01223 352 339

UNIFEM works to ensure the participation of women in all levels of development planning and practice, and acts as a catalyst within the UN system, supporting efforts that link the needs and concerns of women to all critical issues on the national, regional and global agendas.

Wages for Housework (WfH)
Cross Roads Women's Centre, 230a Kentish Town Road, London NW6 5QU Tel: 020 7482 2496
Fax: 020 7209 4761 Email:100010.2311@compuserve.com

WfH is an international, multi-racial network which campaigns for the recognition and compensation for all unwaged work done by women. They are involved in measuring and valuing unwaged work in national accounts. Co-ordinates the international Women Count Network and the Campaign against the Child Support Act.

Women's Environmental Network (WEN)
87 Worship Street, London EC2A 2BE
Tel: 020 7247 3327 Fax: 020 7247 4740
Email: wenuk@gn.apc.org
Website: www.gn.apc.org/wen

WEN works to ensure that women are empowered to participate in local decision-making processes, especially through Local Agenda 21. The network campaigns on health issues such as breast cancer and toxic shock syndrome. They also produce briefings on issues such as green parenting, chocolate and cleaning products.

Women's National Commission
Cabinet Office, 4th Floor, Horse Guards Road, London SW1P 3AL Tel: 020 7238 0386 Fax: 020 7238 0387
Email: v.patel@cabinet-office.gov.uk

The Women's National Commission is the official, independent, advisory body that works to ensure that women's views are both taken into account by the Government and heard in public debate. It has 50 full and over 30 associate member organisations drawn from the major political parties, trade unions, religious groups, professional associations and voluntary bodies, representing all parts of the UK.

Inspiring and enabling young people

'Treat the world well. It was not given to you by your parents – it was willed to you by your children'

Kenyan proverb

YOUNG PEOPLE ARE 30% OF THE WORLD'S POPULATION. It is obvious that they should participate in decisions that affect their future. Young people across the world need a healthy environment, improved living standards, education, and employment opportunities.

'Governments ... should establish procedures for allowing consultation and possible participation of youth in decision-making processes with regard to the environment, involving youth at the local, national and regional levels.'

Agenda 21, Chapter 25

The right of young people to have a voice in environmental decisions which affect them now is enshrined in Agenda 21, which also stresses the importance of local action. This is particularly relevant for young people for whom their local environment most impacts on their quality of life. It is likely to be where young people feel most comfortable and can therefore feel most empowered to take action.

Agenda 21 also requires that young people should be involved 'in project identification, design, implementation and follow-up'. This means there is an opportunity for teachers and youth workers to work with local authorities, other NGOs, and within their own organisations, to facilitate youth participation in sustainable development issues. This encompasses a need to provide support for young people's views, and develop projects which promote skill-sharing and empowerment of young people as agents of change.

Yet many young people assume that their views or suggestions for change will be ignored or dismissed. This is a challenge that any new project may need to face. Feedback indicates the most rewarding events or programmes are developed and continue when young people are empowered to achieve a specific project goal and/or liaise with those in positions of authority such as local councillors.

More and more local authorities are open to suggestions from community and youth organisations and are funding events for young people on sustainable development issues such as conferences and youth committees. This is often dependent on youth workers or teachers offering specific ideas for projects or programmes. There are an increasing number of small grants available for community-based activities either singly or in partnership with the local authority or other local organisations.

Initiatives from within the youth work and voluntary sector tend to encourage young people to evolve their *own* projects and carry them through. There are also a growing number of training opportunities for youth workers and those wishing to work with young people specifically on issues of sustainable development. Organisations such as the Royal Society for the Protection of Birds (RSPB), British Trust for Conservation Volunteers (BTCV) and Wildlife Trusts have established youth membership programmes and, through them, particular projects in which they encourage their young members to become involved.

Many local projects involving young people in community action, or environment projects in schools are already working on or toward the wider issues of sustainable development. Youth groups and schools will be able to build on work they are already doing or widen the scope of their existing work with young people to include sustainable development issues.

Key organisations

British Trust for Conservation Volunteers (BTCV)
36 St Mary's Street, Wallingford, Oxfordshire OX10 IEU Tel: 01491 839766

BTCV offer placements for young people of all ages in practical conservation projects in both rural and urban environments. Youth groups can affiliate and receive training.

British Youth Council
65–69 White Lion Street, London N1 9PP
Tel: 020 7278 0582 Fax: 020 7278 05833

BYC represents almost all national voluntary youth and student organisations in the UK, and puts young people's views forward to government. It is active in the promotion of political education, development of local youth councils and in other participation projects.

Centre for Alternative Technology (CAT)
(see Main organisations)

Council for Environmental Education (CEE)
(see Main organisations)

CEE's Youth Unit produces information, resources and a regular newsletter supporting those involved or wanting to become involved in environmental youth work.

Eco-Schools
c/o Tidy Britain Group, The Pier, Wigan WN3 4EX
Tel: 01942 82 4620

Eco-Schools is a national programme helping schools to take environmental lessons from the classroom and applying them to the day-to day running of the school through a programme of activities.

Groundwork Foundation (see Main organisations)
Many Groundwork Trusts around the UK work actively with local children and young people.

Living Earth
4 Great James Street, London WC1N 3DA
Tel: 020 7242 3816

Living Earth is an educational charity working with schools, local businesses, volunteers groups, local authorities and Parent–Teacher Associations to develop partnerships for long-term action on local issues of sustainability. The 'My Place Our Place' scheme aims to encourage schools to develop project ideas and apply for grants for carrying these ideas through.

Rescue Mission: Planet Earth
Peace Child International, The White House, Buntingford, Herts. SG9 9AH
Tel: 01763 27 4459 Fax: 01763 27 4460
Email: rescuemission@compuserve.com
Website: www.peacechild.org

Rescue Mission is an international organisation seeking to make Agenda 21 understandable, and empower young people to take action. It encourages young people to find out about and monitor progress on the sustainability of their local community through their Indicators Pack, available for secondary/college and primary levels. Recent projects also include 'Stand up for your rights', a youth version of the UN Declaration on Human Rights.

StudentForce for Sustainability
Brewery House, Ketton, Stamford PE9 3TA
Tel: 01780 720172 Fax: 01780 722072
Email: sfs@studentforce.demon.co.uk
Website: www.studentforce.demon.co.uk

StudentForce engages students and recent graduates in partnership with businesses, communities and local authorities. Project work includes rural sustainable regeneration, community and business development, environmental audits, energy efficiency for householders and businesses, Local Agenda 21 and much else. All parties have the opportunity to learn new skills together.

WATCH
c/o RSNC, The Wildlife Trusts, The Kiln, Waterside, Mather Road, Newark NG24 1WT Tel: 01636 677711
Fax: 01636 670001 Email: info@wildlife-trusts.cix.co.uk
Website: www.wildlifetrust.org.uk

WATCH is the junior wing of the Wildlife Trusts and has local groups which undertake wildlife projects. The Wildlife Trusts are also initiating a 'Children for Change' programme which will enable children and young people aged 8–13 to make decisions about what the crucial issues are in their local environment, gain confidence to take positive action, and link with the local community.

Woodcraft Folk
England and Wales: 13 Ritherdon Road, London SW17 8QE Tel: 020 8672 6031
Scotland: 95 Morrison Street, Glasgow G5 8LP
Tel: 0141 304 5552

The Woodcraft Folk are a youth network that developed as an alternative to the Scouting movement. They have a strong environmental focus.

Youth Clubs UK
Kirby House, 20–24 Kirby Street, London EC1N 8TS
Tel: 020 7242 4045

Youth Clubs UK have a Peer Environmental Education Programme (PEEP) which encourages youth groups to establish specific programmes.

Further information

The Ass Kickers Guide to the Galaxy is a lively introduction to sustainable development highlighting the issues, lifestyle changes, practical action and campaigning suggestions. Youth Clubs UK, 1995.

Eco Warrior's Handbook and *Fuming Mad* are Friends of the Earth (FoE) publications which provide information on specific issues and what young people can do individually or as a group.

Environmental Ethnic Youth Work: first year report 1996–97 Black Environment Network, 1998. Report on the Ethnic Youth Work Development Projects in London and Nottingham which includes concerns expressed by ethnic young people and community groups, obstacles to participation and feedback on the projects from participants.

Let's Grasp the Nettle (ages 9–13); *Let's Take the World in Hand* (ages 13–16) Environmental Packs which cover a range of topics using games and practical activities in both urban and rural settings. Available from the Woodcraft Folk.

Rescue Mission Planet Earth: a children's edition of Agenda 21 Rescue Mission, 1994. This young people's version of Agenda 21 brings sustainable development issues into lively focus for young people and offers views of those issues from young people in many parts of the world.

Youth Action and the Environment Council for Environmental Education, 1997. Contains many excellent working examples of youth projects around the UK. It also contains information about sustainable development, groups activities and information on available written material.

Website

Newham Council have organised several young people's conferences on the environment. They have a web site for young people to discuss issues which are important to them including environmental concerns and activities: www.youth.newham.org.uWime5

● Educational groups

THE KEY ROLE OF EDUCATION in the process of working towards sustainable development is highlighted in *Agenda 21*:

> *'Education is critical for promoting sustainable development and improving the capacity of the people to address environment and development issues. It is also critical for achieving environmental and ethical awareness, values and attitudes, skills and behaviour consistent with sustainable development and effective public participation in decision-making.'*
>
> **Agenda 21, Chapter 36:**
> **Promoting education, public awareness and training**

THIS CONTRIBUTION HAS LONG BEEN ACKNOWLEDGED and promoted by NGOs and others working in the fields of environment and education, nationally and internationally:

> *'Sustainable living must be the new pattern for all levels: individuals, communities, nations and the world. To adopt the new pattern will require a significant change in the attitudes and practices of many people. We will need to ensure that education programmes reflect the importance of an ethic for living sustainably and that information campaigns are mounted to disseminate it.'*
>
> **International Union for the Conservation of Nature, United Nations Environment Programme and World Wide Fund for Nature, *Caring for the Earth: A Strategy for Sustainable Living*, 1991**

Education for sustainable development has its roots in environmental education, which has evolved since the 1960s, and development education, which first emerged in the 1970s. It links with other related approaches to education which stress relevance to personal, social, economic and environmental change. These approaches have increasingly found commonality under the label of 'education for sustainable development' and there is a strengthening consensus about the meaning and implications of this approach for education as a whole.

Numerous ministerial statements over the last ten years have stressed the importance of this work, including a joint Department for Education and Employment (DfEE) and Department of the Environment (DoE, now DETR) conference in 1995, the *Government Strategy for Environmental Education* (1996) and the recent establishment of the Panel on Education for Sustainable Development.

> *'Environmental education is a central means of furthering the Government's commitment to sustainable development. It gives people that capacity to address environmental issues which is vital to achieving a sustainable society.'*
>
> **Taking environmental education into the 21st century: the Government's strategy for environmental education in England, 1996**

In addition, the Government's commitment to sustainable development and to the role of education in working towards a sustainable society, is manifest in the revised *UK Sustainable Development Strategy 1999* and in the Department for International Development White Paper, 'Eliminating World Poverty' (1998).

The Government Panel on Education for Sustainable Development was set up in 1998 to consider issues on education for sustainable development in its broadest sense in schools, further and higher education, at work, during recreation and at home; and to make recommendations for action in England. The Panel (which has a five-year life) is chaired by Sir Geoffrey Holland and has 23 members. It reports annually to the Deputy Prime Minister and Secretary of State for Education and Employment setting out recommendations for action by Government, the Panel and other key players.

Objectives of the Panel on Education for Sustainable Development

1. To promote a strategic approach to sustainable development education in England.
2. To identify gaps and opportunities in the provision of sustainable development education and consider how to improve that provision.
3. To promote an approach which will reduce duplication, increase co-operation and develop synergy between all sectors and groups involved.
4. To consider whether and what targets should be set for various sectors.
5. To highlight best practice and consider the means of disseminating it more widely.
6. To make recommendations to key players on priority areas for action.
7. To assess the effectiveness of this approach.

The Panel has set up sectoral sub-groups to address the needs of key groups: schools, further and higher education, the workplace, and general public. In September 1998 the Panel submitted its report on education for sustainable development in the schools sector to DfEE and the Qualifications and Curriculum Authority (QCA). The report identifies generic learning outcomes for each of seven key concepts of sustainable development. The Panel also recommends that every school should have regard to sustainable development within its overall school policy.

Local authorities (in particular through the Local Agenda 21 process) and the new Regional Government offices are also addressing education and awareness as part of their work on sustainable development. Other partnership initiatives, such as Local Biodiversity Action Plans, also recognise the key role of education and awareness in ensuring long-term progress towards sustainable development.

In March 1999 DfEE and DETR launched a code to promote new standards for environmental education resources issued by companies and organisations. The code, developed in consultation with 400 organisations, hinges around ten principles of good practice. These include a requirement that environmental information is accurate, current and verifiable with careful consideration being given to identifying a need to produce such material in the first place. The Code will be monitored by the Council for Environmental Education.

Key organisations

Council for Environmental Education (CEE)
94 London Street, Reading, Berks. RG1 4SJ
Tel: 0118 950 2550 Email: info@cee.i-way.co.uk
Website: www.cee.org.uk

CEE provides a national focus for environmental education and a voice for those committed to education for sustainable development. It aims to ensure that the principles of sustainable development are at the heart of education policy and practice.

Development Education Association
3rd Floor, 29–31 Cowper Street, London EC2A 4AP
Tel: 020 7490 8108 Email: devedassoc@gn.apc.org

Going for Green (see Main organisations)

WWF (see Main organisations)
The WorldWide Fund for Nature have a substantial education department and do a great deal of work on community education and education for sustainability. They produce a termly teachers newsletter and an annual resources catalogue, as well as having much material on the website.

Relevant publications

Caring for the earth: a strategy for sustainable living Munro, David and Holdgate, Martin (eds), International Union for Conservation of Nature and Natural Resources/United Nations Environment Programme/WWF, 1991

Children's participation: the theory and practice of involving young citizens in community development and environmental care Hart, Roger, Earthscan, 1996

Code on Education for Sustainable Development 1999. Available from DETR Free Literature or on the Website at www.detr.gov.uk

Educating for a sustainable local authority, Local Agenda 21 Roundtable Guidance Note 4, Local Government Management Board (now IdeA), 1995

Education for sustainability, Huckle, John and Sterling, Stephen (eds), Earthscan, 1996

Education for sustainable development in the schools sector: a report to DfEE/QCA from the Panel on Education for Sustainable Development, 1998

Shaping education for the 21st century: Agenda for action 1998–2001, Council for Environmental Education, 1998

Strengthening the role of the education community in support of sustainable development, UNED-UK Education for Sustainability Forum, 1997

Sustainable Development Education Panel First Annual Report 1998, DETR, 1999

Taking environmental education into the 21st century: the Government's strategy for environmental education for England, DoE/DfEE, 1996

● Business

'Integration of environmental thinking into the mainstream of decision-making relating to agriculture, trade, investment, research and development, infrastructure and finance is now the best chance for effective action.'

Global Environment Outlook, UNEP, September 1999

'CORPORATIONS, BECAUSE THEY ARE THE DOMINANT INSTITUTION ON THE PLANET, must squarely address the social and environmental problems that affect humankind.' (Hawken 1993) Whilst many are engaged in trying to integrate social, ethical and environmental principles, there is growing recognition that success will be elusive 'until the institutions surrounding commerce are re-designed' too.

Over the last decade consumer, market and legislative pressures have forced many companies to take measures to improve their environmental performance. Environmental pressures on manufacturing now reach into the heart of the industrial process, and slowly but surely, the principles of sustainability are filtering down to the mainstream business community.

The UK Government intends that 'sustainable development will be the key economic driver, introducing new processes and products. Innovation and creativity will be the way we can meet the challenge of competitiveness ... Firms will have to find ways to get more from less. Production and distribution systems will have to change to reduce emissions, resource use and waste.' Areas of work will include: cutting energy consumption; increasing materials' efficiency; adopting cleaner production, producer responsibility, eco-design, and purchasing strategies supportive of environmental and social concerns.

Principle 16 of the Rio Declaration highlights the important role economic instruments could play in assisting this transition. Examples include fiscal instruments such as taxes on inputs, exports, pollution and resources, and loans, grants, subsidies and 'green funds'. Other instruments encompass tradeable emission permits, land permits and catch quotas. The Landfill Tax was the UK's first green tax and has already had an impact.

Corporate social responsibility

Improving environmental management is a first step. The bigger questions are about the role of business in achieving a sustainable economy. There are calls for new values and attitudes, and wider transparency to underpin corporate strategies. For example, just how can the external perception of a company's values and its internal practices be matched up? What is needed to create and sustain leadership and ethics in business?

Corporate social responsibility and accountability are increasingly seen as strategic business issues. This marks the shift from what Shell has described as 'trust me' through 'tell me' to 'show me' modes of communication. These demand new processes involving a wider group of stakeholders to increase awareness and promote understanding. Such approaches also demand better access to information.

Seeking 'good practice'

There is much talk of 'good practice' although there is also uncertainty over the criteria used to define such practice. Projects may cover:

- environmental sustainability – in managing energy, transport, waste and pollution
- social sustainability – greening of trading, investment and service industries, and enhanced responsibility to all stakeholders including suppliers, employees, customers, the public and future generations
- economic sustainability – self reliance, local equity and diversity of economy and workforce.

'Green business' clubs are springing up all over the country, many backed by the DTI Environmental Technology Best Practice Programme or linked into academic institutions. The promotion of waste minimisation initiatives and environmental management schemes is fundamental to their work.

Producer responsibility

The first UK 'producer responsibility' legislation is the 1997 Packaging Waste Regulations. The aim is to put the 'polluter pays' principle into practice by ensuring that companies handling substantial quantities of packaging take responsibility for their products throughout their entire life cycle, including disposal. Extended producer responsibility is a new and promising policy tool because it finally moves away from just looking at waste and considers the whole life cycle impacts of the product. Moreover, the focus is on prevention, instead of the traditional control approach.

Cleaner production

This involves the redesign of industrial products and processes to minimise resource use, waste and emissions to the environment. Cleaner production has proved highly profitable financially and environmentally. It has clear links with sustainable consumption. This was defined by the Oslo Symposium (1994) as 'the use of goods and services that respond to basic needs and bring a better quality of life, while minimising the use of natural resources, toxic materials and emissions of waste and pollutants over the life cycle, so as not to jeopardise the needs of future generations'.

Increasing materials' efficiency

'Doing more with less is not the same as doing less, doing worse or doing without. Efficiency does not mean curtailment, discomfort or privation...'

E. Weizsacker, A Lovins. Authors of Factor Four – Doubling Wealth, Halving Resource Use, 1997

Eco-efficiency measures based around Factor four (and the more radical Factor ten) concepts propose that businesses can be four times more efficient in their use of resources than they are currently, and that they can do it using currently available technologies. In other words, it is not technical innovation that is required but fresh thinking.

Environmental management systems

Voluntary management systems are helping moves towards sustainable industrial development and can help improve corporate environmental performance and public accountability. EMAS is a voluntary EU Regulation, applicable to sites in Europe with industrial activities. Performance-based, EMAS aims to 'prevent, reduce and as far as possible eliminate pollution, particularly at source on the basis of the polluter pays principle, to ensure sound management of resources and to use clean or cleaner technology...'

ISO14001 – an International Environmental Management Systems Standard – is less rigorous, but there is still relatively little action. One survey suggests that many firms are sitting on the fence. They are putting environmental systems into place and establishing what it takes to obtain ISO14001 if it ever becomes essential, but there is no trend towards ISO14001 certification. Positive benefits include 'greening the supply chain' and efforts to use public and private sector purchasing power to bring about change.

Ethical banking and financial services

This sector is viewed as a growth business allowing people to put their money where their beliefs are. It is being boosted by the Government's requirement that from July 2000 the trustees of all UK pension schemes will have to disclose 'the extent to which social, environmental or ethical considerations are taken into account in the selection, retention and realisation of investments'.

Ethical and fair trade initiatives

Fair-trade initiatives are also developing rapidly. Fair trade enables small-scale farmers, producers and communities involved in growing and producing products to receive a fair return for their labour. In turn their communities benefit from the greater economic security and improved health and education that long-term and fair initiatives can bring.

Within this sector, new ways of working and alternative visions of work are developing. Many ventures are co-operatives or seek to integrate spiritual values into successful business initiatives. The latter includes the notion of the Buddhist 'Right Livelihood' – earning a living without doing harm, whether physical, psychological, ethical or spiritual, to any living being.

Key organisations

Advisory Committee on Business and the Environment (ACBE)
Website: www.dti.gov.uk/ACBE8

ACBE comprises senior industrialists who report directly to Government to provide a strategic dialogue with business on environmental issues. Working groups produce reports on specific topics. The 8th Report (1998) contained 50 recommendations to help stimulate positive business action on issues ranging from climate change and transport policy to sustainable consumption and the use of water resources.

British Standards Institution (BSI)
389 Chiswick High Road, London W4 4AL
Tel: 020 8996 9001 Fax: 020 8996 7001
Email: info@bsi.org.uk

BSI has formed a new group on sustainability seeking to integrate environmental, health and safety, social and ethical management into a coherent framework. It is also participating in a DTI Project 'A Framework for Sustainable Business – Towards the Next Generation of Management Systems'.

Business in the Environment (BiE)
44 Baker Street, London W1M 1DH Tel: 020 7224 1600
Fax: 020 7486 1700 Email: bie@bitc.org.uk
Website: www.business-in-environment.org.uk

BiE is part of Business in the Community, which works to increase the corporate sector's involvement in community activities and to increase social responsibility by encouraging companies to give practical support to the voluntary sector. BiE was established to promote business–community partnerships and practical steps to help businesses improve their environmental performance. It promotes green business clubs and publishes a UK environmental business club directory.

DTI–UK Eco-efficiency Initiative (UKEEI)
Website: www.dti.gov.uk/ukeei

Part of the UK's contribution to the World Business Council for Sustainable Development/European Partners for the Environment (WBCSD/EPE) European Eco-Efficiency initiative. The new DTI website includes information on eco-efficiency activities in the UK, thus providing a 'one-stop virtual shop' for business.

Energy Efficiency Best Practice Programme (EEBPP)
Tel: 0800 512012

A government initiative providing free advice to companies with regard to energy savings and competitiveness. In addition, Energy Efficiency Advice Centres provide free and independent advice to businesses.

Environmental Technology Support Unit (ETSU)
Website: www.etsu.co.uk

ETSU is a joint DTI and DETR sponsored service that provides environmental advice and support to industry. The website introduces the extensive range of ETSU's free services plus a good list of case studies (Environmental Technology Best Practice Programme (ETBPP)).

Ethical Property Company plc (EPC)
43 St Giles, Oxford, OX1 3LW Tel: 01865 316338
Fax: 01865 516288 Email: epc@centres.demon.co.uk
Website: www.centres.demon.co.uk

EPC is working to build a national network of action centres around the UK providing affordable rent, office space and shared facilities for charities, campaign groups and co-operatives working to secure positive social change and a sustainable future.

Forum for the Future (see Environmental organisations)

Groundwork (see Main organisations)

National Centre for Business and Ecology (NCBE)
The Peel Building, University of Salford, Greater Manchester M5 4WT Tel: 0161 295 5276
Fax: 0161 295 5041 Email: NCBE@NCBE.salford.ac.uk
Website: www.NCBE.co.uk

Inspired and set up by the Co-operative Bank, the NCBE offers practical and focused sustainable solutions to a range of businesses and organisations in four broad service areas: strategic sustainable policy; social responsibility; applied environmental solutions; and support for the environmental improvement of small businesses.

New Economics Foundation
(see Main organisations)

Prince of Wales Business Leaders Forum
15–16 Cornwall Terrace, Regent's Park, London NW1 4QP Tel: 020 7467 3656 Fax: 020 7467 3610
Email: info@pwblf Website: www.pwblf.org

This network of global business leaders and corporations has been promoting corporate social responsibility since 1990. Work includes the International Hotels Environment Initiative encouraging continuous improvement in the environmental performance of this major service industry and a new millennium initiative exploring the values that underpin and guide the activities of companies striving to be good corporate citizens in the 21st century.

Social Venture Network Europe
46–48 Grosvenor Gardens, London SW1W 0EB
Tel: 020 7881 9007 Fax: 020 7881 9008
Website: www.svneurope.com

A group of socially and environmentally responsible businesses, organisations and individuals concerned with the changing role of business in a global economy.

Training and Enterprise Councils (TECs)
TEC National Council Tel: 020 7735 0010

Local TECs often run schemes that financially assist companies in making environmental improvements.

Triodos Bank
Brunel House, 11 The Promenade, Bristol BS8 3NN
Tel: 0117 973 9339 (local call rate number 0345 697239)
Fax: 0117 973 9303 Email: mail@triodos.co.uk

An independent bank, Triodos lends only to projects and enterprises which create social and environmental value – in fields such as renewable energy, social housing, complementary health care, fair trade, organic food, farming and socially aware business ventures. Triodos also forges specific partnerships and links with organisations by offering ethical savings accounts, for example the Soil Association and Quaker Social Housing through its Organic Saver Account and its Just Housing Account, which targets innovative social housing.

World Business Council for Sustainable Development
160, route de Florissant, Ch-1231 Conches-Geneva, Switzerland Tel: +41 22 839 3100 Fax: +41 22 839 3131

A coalition of 120 international companies sharing a commitment to the environment and to the principles of economic growth and sustainable development. Its mission is to provide business leadership as a catalyst for change towards sustainable development and to promote the attainment of eco-efficiency through high standards of environmental and resource management in business.

Publications

Better Business Pack. World-Wide Fund for Nature (WWF-UK)/NatWest Group Better Business Programme Tel: 01483 426444 or visit website: www.wrf-uk.org/education/betbus

Provides help to companies to make financial performance improvements at the same time as reducing their impact on the environment. The full pack is a self-help guide based on the experience of more than 160 small and medium-size firms and contains a money-back guarantee if the plans implemented don't save money. A Quick Start Guide is available free of charge.

Business and the Environment – The Earthscan reader edited by R. Welford and R. Starkey. 1996. Earthscan, London

Deep Change or Slow Death: What future for business? ERP Environment Briefings No 3 and *Creating the Sustainable Business: A Buddhist path*. Briefing No 2 £7.50 each, PO Box 75, Shipley, West Yorkshire BD17 6EZ Tel: 01274 530408 Website: www.erpenvironment.org

Two thought-provoking briefings arguing for new values and ethics in business. The first argues that until individuals change, businesses are limited by human greed. But businesses can and will change if individuals can sort out their own priorities and recognise that 'less is more'. The second briefing considers spiritual dimensions in both business and sustainable development and sets out a path of transformation based on a Buddhist approach leading to more sustainable business.

ENDS (Environmental Data Services): Tel: 020 7814 5300 Fax: 020 7415 0106 Email: post@ends.co.uk

Services include a monthly newsletter on latest developments in environmental management and regulation and on-line information, including a daily environmental briefing.

Environment Business: Tel: 020 7654 7111 Fax: 020 8944 2930 Email: ebnb@ifi.co.uk Website: www.ifi.co.uk

Produces a fortnightly newsletter, briefings, magazine, various directories and electronic information.

Mapping the Maze: A directory of essential environmental legislation for small business managers in Wales and England. L. Connell, R. Bayliss, A. Flynn and M. Adebowale. £7.50 (plus £1.50 postage) Copies from ELF Tel: 020 7404 1030.

Published by the Environmental Law Foundation (ELF) and Cardiff University, this guide is aimed at managers in small businesses in the manufacturing, processing, legal and service sectors in Wales and England taking their first steps in environmental improvement. It avoids legal jargon, uses checklists and simple steps, and steers firms towards further sources of help.

The Ecology of Commerce – A declaration of sustainability. Paul Hawken. 1993. Phoenix, London.

Described as a springboard for a radical new way of looking at ecology in the commercial world, Hawken's book remains a provocative contribution to the debate.

● Trade unions

'Trade unions are vital actors in facilitating the achievement of sustainable development in view of their experience in addressing industrial change, the extremely high priority they give to protection of the working environment and the related natural environment.'

Agenda 21, Chapter 29

A WELL KNOWN ACADEMIC has asserted that 'historically the trade union movement was essentially an environmental protest movement' (Pepper, 1995) improving the living and working conditions of millions of people. The development of a more sustainable community has always been a central plank of trade union priorities when tackling questions of health and safety, poverty, equity, and justice. In a more modern context, unions have spearheaded very significant environmental campaigns, such as: The Transport & General Workers' Union's (T&G) campaign to ban the chemical 2-4-5-T and the campaign by the National Union of Seamen to ban the dumping of nuclear waste at sea, which have had effects far beyond the workplace.

Local Agenda 21 has given the trade union movement a perfect opportunity to play an active part with the local community to provide a voice for the ordinary working population. The identification of the trade union movement as a major group (see Chapter 29, Agenda 21) realises the potential role of trade unions in sustainable development. Trade unions provide an independent voice of the workplace whilst at the same time being an organisation firmly rooted in the community. Trade unions also have access to many people who have not traditionally been involved in sustainable development issues. If enhanced, this could be a valuable route for dialogue between workers (and their communities) and environmental organisations. Trade unions such as the T&G have held a long-standing commitment to a constructive dialogue between environmental organisations and themselves with policies such as 'We will also work positively with organisations in this area with whom we share common objectives,' cited in a 1989 policy booklet *Forward T&G*.

The most immediate possibility for trade unions' involvement in sustainable development issues is through the workplace with the attachment of the environment to health and safety problems. This locates environmental issues soundly within the trade union remit. The practical applications of this proposal are currently being researched by the Trade Unions and Sustainable Development Advisory Committee. However, with this association established, trade unions can negotiate the application of environmental protection to the conventional monitoring and inspection role of the trade union-recognised health and safety representative. This utilises the first-hand knowledge that workers have of dangerous forms of production. Trade union activists can also have an invaluable role in the implementation and monitoring of the environmental management systems such as ISO14001. This also illustrates an inherent dilemma for a worker: the need for waged work, and the potentially negative environmental consequences arising from employment.

Trade unions also have an important educational role. Region 1 of the T&G and the University of North London (UNL), for example, now offer a unique programme of environmental education for trade union members. These courses allow trade union members to develop ideas of sustainability beyond their own workplace and into the community as a whole.

Beyond the workplace

There are further important initiatives involving wider sustainability issues. One is the applying of pressure through trade union pension trustees for ethical and environmentally sensitive investment and the purchase of shares to enable the raising of environmental/ethical issues with other shareholders at AGMs. This wider workplace context encompasses traditional routes of lobbying for extensions to existing legislation to include a statutory framework for trade union involvement in environmental regulation at work.

Trade unions have been actively involved in recent environmental campaigns. All three major transport unions support the 'Don't Choke Britain' traffic reduction initiative, as does public sector union Unison, which has also been actively involved in developing policy work on environment and health issues.

British trade unions also need to link their workplace to the wider world. Canada provides a useful model for what can be achieved through a sustainable development agenda. The Green Work Alliance, established in 1991, had the primary aim of reopening a Caterpillar plant in Toronto. This initiative was inspired by the efforts of a shop stewards combine and the work of the T&G who, in 1976 and 1983, proposed far-reaching changes to convert Lucas Aerospace (UK) to a socially/environmentally sustainable industry. The impetus for the Canadian project was to open a plant dedicated to environmentally friendly production and, to further their objectives, an alliance was established with local green groups and the wider community. The initiatives of this experiment have been sustained and a dialogue is maintained between the labour and environmental movements.

Key organisations

Trades Union Congress
Congress House, Great Russell Street, London WC1B 3LS Tel: 020 7636 4030 Fax: 020 7636 0632
Website: www.tuc.org.uk

Publications

Many of these ideas and activities can be followed up in the sources cited below.

Trade Unions as Environmental Actors: A Case Study of the Transport & General Workers' Union, Mason, M. and Morter, N., 1999 in Mason, M. *Environmental Democracy*, Earthscan, 1999

Workplace Pollution Reduction TGWU, 1999

Pesticide Reduction TGWU, 1997

Eco-Auditing TGWU, 1996

Clean Production: From Industrial Dinosaur to Eco-Efficiency Gee, D. MSF, 1994

Greening the Workplace Trade Union Congress, TUC, 1991

Trade Union Action: A Paradigm for Sustainable Development, Gereluk, W. & Royer, L, 1997 in Dodds, F. *The Way Forward: Beyond Agenda 21*, Earthscan, 1997

● The arts and local sustainability

THE UK HAS A STRONG TRADITION OF ARTISTS that work in the community. In recent years many UK arts institutions have made significant headway into developing wider access to their work through programmes of community outreach and education. The arts, as a sector, however has not been deeply involved in planning for sustainable development. But the arts have qualities that can be useful in planning sustainable communities, contributing to personal and social development as well as serving as a vehicle through which people learn about the environment, heritage and other issues.

A sustainable future depends on our ability to learn, to innovate, to solve problems and, most importantly, to educate our children to be the adaptive and flexible agents of change who can make the 21st century work. Our ability to do this depends upon the tenacity, morality and vitality with which we make use of our creative capacities; and the arts, in all of their forms and locations, should be part of the team that helps us do this.

The place to look for the arts, including design, that are involved in sustainable development is anywhere that artists and designers (and the institutions and funders that support them) are striving to make connections between the arts and human development: the arts and environment; the arts and health; the arts and community development; and the arts and education. Through such collaborations, the arts are making themselves more accessible and more available for non-artists to use as tools with which to explore and develop creative skills of their own.

Art, communities and sustainability

Community arts organisations are the most logical places to begin to map where the arts connect with sustainable development. Community arts groups in the UK are acknowledged by many as being among the most sophisticated in the world. Led by organisations such as Free Form, Common Ground, Green Candle Dance Company, Heads Together and Magic Me, community artists have worked outside the safety of the studio and directly with people in communities. These artists act as animators by helping people engage in art processes to develop their creative impulses.

In recent years, several new network/placement organisations have come into existence which advocate and develop connections between particular art forms and the community. The basis of these organisations is participation and quality of experience. Foremost among such organisations are Sound Sense and the Foundation for Community Dance. Sound Sense is a national development agency for participatory music-making in the community. It has a music and disability advice service; it runs courses and maintains a network for the sharing of skills, knowledge and information. It publishes an excellent magazine, *Sounding Board*. The Foundation for Community Dance produces *Animated*, a quarterly magazine, as part of its aim to create greater access to and participation in dance in community contexts. The Foundation is in the process of conducting a national mapping project to be fully informed of such activity throughout the country.

The Foundation and Sound Sense are also involved in promoting connection with health workers, and offer advice on preparing applications to the National Lottery's New Opportunities Fund for Healthy Living Centres. Both organisations promote the use of their art forms in healthcare, not as therapy, but in and of themselves, since it is clear that participation in the making of music and dance brings benefits: helping to empower people, creating positive attitudes, building confidence, providing skills, developing community and social cohesion and aiding personal development.

A number of hybrid sectors have grown up to help place the arts into a development context. Among these are arts and urban design, public art, cultural districts, and the cultural industries. There are others more closely related to environmental concerns. Some of these have come from an environmental perspective: Common Ground are perhaps the best known. They work with community groups to produce records of their communities, often known as Parish Maps, that can become works of art in their own right. Other organisations such as Groundwork are incorporating community art in environmental projects.

The Centre for Creative Communities, based in London, has its roots in the arts, but promotes creative development in communities anchored in shared values and mutual understanding. The arts are a particularly rich contributor to this kind of development because they have qualities that help people to develop intelligences beyond those normally acquired in school. The arts:

- enhance creative thinking and problem solving ability
- increase communication skills
- enhance basic literacy skills
- develop self-esteem and help people gain a positive self image
- provide people with better cross-cultural understanding.

Key organisations

Centre for Creative Communities
118 Commercial Street, London E1 6NF
Tel: 020 7247 5385 Fax: 020 7247 5256
Email: baaa@easynet.co.uk
Website: www.creativecommunities.org.uk

Common Ground (see Main organisations)

Foundation for Community Dance
Cathedral Chambers, 2 Peacock Lane, Leicester
LE1 5PR Tel: 0116 251 0516 Fax: 0116 251 0517
Email: comdanceinc@easynet.co.uk

Free Form Arts Trust
38 Dalston Lane, London E8 3AZ Tel: 020 7249 3394

Green Candle Dance Company
224 Aberdeen House, 22 Highbury Grove, London
N5 2DQ Tel: 020 7359 8776 Fax: 020 7359 5840
Email: greencandle@compuserve.com

Heads Together
32 Metheley Terrace, Leeds LS7 3PB
Tel: 0973 172433 Fax: 0113 262 9223
Email: adrian@heads.demon.co.uk

Magic Me
118 Commercial Street, London E1 6NF
Tel: 020 7375 0961 Fax: 020 7247 5256

Sound Sense
Riverside House, Rattlesden, Bury St Edmunds
IP30 0SF Tel/Fax: 01449 73 7649
Email: 100256.30@compuserve.com

Publications

Other magazines that address relevant connections between the community and the arts include *Mailout*, *VAN Update*, and *95%*. *Mailout* follows developments at the interface between the arts and the community in a variety of settings; *VAN Update* is the membership magazine for the Voluntary Arts Network; and *95%* serves as a voice for youth arts.

95% Available from Youth Arts Network, Weston Corner, Station Road, Fladbury, Worcs WR10 2QW Tel/Fax: 01386 86 0390
Email: yan.youthclubs.uk@ukonline.co.uk

Sounding Board (see **Sound Sense** above)

Interchanges (see **Centre for Creative Communities** above)

VAN Update: Available from the Voluntary Arts Network, PO Box 200, Cardiff CF5 1YH
Tel: 01222 39 5395 Fax: 01222 39 7397
Email: info@vanmail.demon.co.uk

● Religion and faith-based organisations

'I claim that human mind or human society is not divided into water-tight compartments, called social, political, religious. I do not believe that the spiritual law works on a field of its own. On the contrary, it expresses itself only through the ordinary activities of life. It thus affects the economic, the social, and the political fields.'

Mahatma Gandhi

POLITICS AND SPIRITUALITY, so often treated as distinctly separate entities, have closer links than many people would like to acknowledge. Despite the decline in the formal expression of faith, socially-engaged commentators still discern an enormous need in the general public for some kind of spiritual fulfilment and spiritual meaning to life. Social action, combined with inner personal change, underpins innovative activity towards sustainable development and contributes to the search for new values that go beyond some of the material confines within which most of our life is pitched.

Religious groups have long been involved in development through organisations such as Christain Aid or CAFOD. New approaches are now emerging in a move away from the traditional Christian 'stewardship' position that the land is there to be 'used' by humans, to a more celebratory, inter-connected view, for example, Christian-centred spirituality. Buddhism is now one of the fastest growing spiritual traditions in the western world. Throughout its 2500 year history it has always succeeded in adapting its mode of expression to suit whatever culture it has encountered. Its emphasis on interconnectedness, harmony of the universe, individual change and compassion and its doctrine of non-violence are all concepts that sit well within the path to greater sustainability.

Key groups

Baha'i Faith
27 Rutland Gate, London SW7 1PD
Tel: 020 7584 2566 Fax: 020 7584 9401

Concerned with social justice and a spiritual involvement of values and world commonwealth, Baha'is believe in a co-relation between the spiritual state of humankind and the social, economic and environmental problems facing the world today.

Catholic Institute for International Relations (CIIR)
Unit 3, Canonbury Yard, 190a New North Road, London N1 7BJ Tel: 020 7354 0883
Email: ciirlon@gn.acp.org Website: www.ciir.org

CIIR tackles the causes of poverty and injustice internationally through advocacy and skill sharing. It works with people of all faiths and none.

Christian Ecology Link
20 Carlton Road, Harrogate HG2 8DD
Tel: 01423 871616 Email: info@christian-ecology.org.uk
Website: www.christian-ecology.org.uk

The national organisation for Christians who care about the environment. It exists to create links between Christian and ecological insights. Members come from various Christian traditions – Anglican, Roman Catholic, Free Church, Quaker. Publishes a quarterly journal, 'Green Christians'.

Eco-Congregation – The Churches Environmental Project
c/o Going for Green, Elizabeth House, The Pier, Wigan WN3 4EX Tel: 01942 612621
Fax: 01942 824778 Email: david@tidybritain.org.uk

A new partnership initiative designed to help churches express their concern for the environment in both practical and spiritual ways.

Friends of the Western Buddhist Order
51 Roman Road, London E2 0HU
Tel: 020 8981 1225 Fax: 020 8980 1960
Website: www.fwbo.org.uk

In living out Buddhist values in the midst of contemporary society, members of the Western Buddhist Order and their friends hope not only to bring about radical change within themselves, but also to effect a change in contemporary life through 'Right Livelihood' and other efforts.

ICOREC – Alliance of Religions and Conservation
3 Wynnstay Grove, Fallowfield, Manchester M14 6XG
Tel: 0161 248 5731 Fax: 0161 248 5736
Email: icorec@icorec.nwnet.co.uk

The Sacred Land Project is a five year scheme aiming to assist local communities, regardless of belief, to conserve, enhance and create sacred spaces. The Project works primarily with sites located in natural and semi-natural environments. Partners include Shell Better Britain and WWF.

Quaker Peace and Service
Contact through local Friends Meeting Houses or through Friends House, 173 Euston Road, London NW1 2BJ Tel: 020 7663 1000 Fax: 020 7663 1001
Website: www.quaker.org.uk

Non-violence is central to the everyday practice of the Friends who have been pioneers in finding ways of bringing about reconciliation and communication between the different 'sides' in important issues.

Part Three

Main organisations and contacts

This part lists organisations that are working on several of the topics in Part 1. It includes key contacts for Scotland, Wales and Northern Ireland and a few regional contacts in England.

Main organisations

Building Research Establishment (BRE)
Bucknalls Lane, Garston, Watford WD2 7JR
Tel: 01923 66 4000 Fax: 01923 66 4010
Email: enquiries@bre.co.uk Website: www.bre.co.uk

BRE is the UK's leading centre for research, development and consultancy for all aspects of the built environment. Various projects cover sustainable buildings, environmentally responsible practices, construction and demolition waste management, re-use and recycling. It runs an online materials exchange. Its new low energy building is designed to be a model for offices of the future and is built from 95% recycled and recovered materials.

Centre for Alternative Technology (CAT)
Machynlleth, Powys, SY20 9AZ
Tel: 01654 702 400 (main) 01654 703 743 (education)
Fax: 01654 702 782 Email: help@catinfo.demon.co.uk
Website: www.cat.org.uk

CAT is a unique demonstration centre designed to inspire, inform and enable society to move towards ecologically sustainable lifestyles. It has become the national centre for information and examples of alternative technology ranging from solar systems to energy efficient building designs and organic growing methods. It publishes a range of information and education material and operates a consultancy service. It is a very popular visitor centre, with the chance to experience more sustainable living and many 'hands-on' exhibits.

Common Ground
PO Box 25309, London NW5 1ZA
Tel/Fax: 020 7267 2144
Website: www.commonground.org.uk

Common Ground is a small organisation that works to emphasise the value of our everyday surroundings and the positive investment people can make in their own localities. It offers ideas, information and inspiration through publications, exhibitions and projects such as Parish Maps, Local Distinctiveness, Apple Day and Community Orchards.

Community Development Foundation (CDF)
60 Highbury Grove, London N5 2AG
Tel: 020 7226 5375 Email: info@cdf.org.uk
Website: www.cdf.org.uk.

CDF pioneers new forms of community development by providing support for community initiatives, promoting best practice, and informing policymakers at local and national level. It has one of the most informative websites around.

Council for Environmental Education (CEE)
94 London Street, Reading RGI 4SJ Tel: 0118 950 2550

CEE promotes and co-ordinates environmental education. Its Youth Unit produces information about national projects and resources and a regular newsletter supporting those involved or wanting to become involved in environmental youth work.

Friends of the Earth (FoE)
26–28 Underwood Street, London N1 7JQ
Tel: 020 7490 1555 Fax: 020 7490 0881
Email: info@foe.co.uk Website: www.foe.co.uk

FoE is one of the largest international networks in the world, with over 50 groups across five continents. FoE England, Wales and Northern Ireland is one of the UK's most influential environmental pressure groups with a unique network of campaigning local groups working in 240 communities throughout England, Wales and Northern Ireland. There is a separate Scottish organisation (see below).

FoE Scotland
72 Newhaven Road, Edinburgh EH6 5QG
Tel: 0131 554 9977 Fax: 0131 554 8656
Email: foescotland@gn.apc.org

Going for Green
Elizabeth House, The Pier, Wigan WN3 4EX
Tel: 01942 612621 Hotline for literature 0800 783 783 8
Fax: 01942 824778 Email: gfg@dircon.co.uk
Website: www.gfg.iclnet.co.uk

Backed by the DETR, this organisation is the principal sustainable development citizen's initiative in the UK for promoting public understanding and involvement in issues relating to sustainable development. Its Sustainable Communities Programme, funded by the National Lottery Charities Board, provides support and opportunities for people to take action locally, addressing their needs and concerns.

Groundwork Foundation
85–87 Cornwall Street, Birmingham B3 3BY
Tel: 0121 236 8565 Fax: 0121 236 7356
Website: www. groundwork.org.uk

Groundwork is a major environmental regeneration charity, active in 150 towns and cities. By working in partnership with the public, private and voluntary sectors, it develops projects that link environmental, social and economic regeneration. Local Groundwork Trusts develop and promote environmental projects in their own localities. Groundwork may be able to offer projects that your group could become involved in or give advice, identify sources funding or offer practical support.

Improvement and Development Association (IdeA) (formerly the Local Government Management Board)
Layden House, 76–86 Turnmill Street, London EC1M 5QU Tel: 020 7296 6600 Fax: 020 7296 6666
Email: local.agenda.21@idea.gov.uk
Website: www.la21-uk.org.uk

(See Local government)

Local Government Association (LGA)

26 Chapter Street, London SW1P 4ND
Tel: 020 7834 2222 Fax: 020 7664 3030
Website: www.lga.gov.uk

The LGA is the representative body for local government and works on all aspects of sustainability in England and Wales, including planning, transport and environment. It has recently issued a position statement on energy services for sustainable communities (1998). This is the most comprehensive argument yet for pursuing sustainable energy strategies at the local and national level.

New Economics Foundation (NEF)

Cinnamon House, 6–8 Cole Street, London SE1 4YH
Tel: 020 7407 7447 Fax: 020 7407 6473
Email: info@neweconomics.org
Website: www.neweconomics.org

NEF arose out of The Other Economic Summit (TOES), which meets around the world parallel to the G7 summit. It researches and promotes local indicators, local currency systems, social auditing, and community banking. Its Centre for Community Visions promotes participation.

Oxfam

Oxfam House, 274 Banbury Road, Oxford OX2 7DZ
Tel: 01865 311311 Fax: 01865 313770
Email: oxfam@oxfam.org.uk

Oxfam works to put an end to poverty world-wide, with an educational and campaigning programme in the UK and Ireland. In partnership with local groups, Oxfam works to tackle powerlessness. It is working with the Social Exclusion Unit to break down stereotypical and negative views of poverty. The Gender and Learning Programme works towards ensuring Oxfam's development and relief programmes make women's lives better. Oxfam's Wastesaver operation in Huddersfield is one of the biggest textile recycling centres in Europe: unsold clothes and textiles raise almost £2 million a year.

Shell Better Britain Campaign

King Edward House, 135a New Street, Birmingham B2 4QJ Tel: 0121 248 5907 Fax: 0121 248 5901
Email: enquiries@sbbc.co.uk Website: www.sbbc.co.uk

Shell Better Britain Campaign encourages action by community groups to improve their local quality of life in ways that are environmentally, socially and economically sustainable. It supports a network of over 25,000 people who are active in their local community. It provides a newsletter and a major information service about local sustainability issues. It awards £250,000 each year to local groups and innovative research projects. Groups are invited join the free Campaign Network.

United Nations Environment and Development – UK Committee (UNED – UK)

3 Whitehall Court, London SW1A 2EL
Tel: 020 7839 1784 Fax: 020 7930 5893
Email: una@mcr1.poptel.org.uk
Website: www.oneworld.org/uned-uk

UNED – UK is a unique network of organisations involved in the process of sustainable development and works to promote environmental protection and sustainable development at the global, national, local and community levels. It works with the UN Environment Programme, the UN Commission for Sustainable Development and other UN processes. UNED-UK contributes to the international policy making process by encouraging activities that result in a multi-sectoral approach and dialogue.

WWF – UK

Panda House, Weyside Park, Godalming, Surrey GU7 1XR Tel: 01483 426444 Fax: 01483 426409
Website: www.wwf-uk.org

WWF is involved in various local sustainability initiatives. It has also addressed the issue of how to engage small and medium size enterprises in the sustainability agenda through the use of 'tool-kits' of resources such as the Better Business pack. It also has a substantial education department and does a great deal of work on community education and education for sustainability. It produces a termly teachers' newsletter and an annual resources catalogue, as well as having much material on the website. WWF is particularly important in providing an international perspective to the debate on biodiversity.

Action across the UK

Scotland

CSV Environment (Scotland)

Centre 21, 236–246 Clyde Street, Glasgow G1 4JH
Tel: 0141 248 6864 Fax: 0141 204 6864
Email: csvgec@gn.apc.org
Website: www.enviroweb.org/greenaction/projects/c21

CSV Environment (Scotland) provides opportunities for those excluded through unemployment, poverty, race or disability to become involved in sustainable development and practical environmental actions. It produces publications, provides support and outreach work to community groups, and develops partnership projects.

Community Self-Build Scotland

72 Newhaven Road, Bonnington Mill, Edinburgh, EH6 5QG Tel: 0131 467 4675 Fax: 0131 538 7223
Email: csbs@ccis.org.uk
Website: www.cableinet.co.uk/users/csbs

An advisory organisation that promotes self-build in an ecological and sustainable manner.

Convention of Scottish Local Authorities (COSLA)
Rosebery House, 9 Haymarket Terrace, Edinburgh EA12 5XZ Tel: 0131 474 9269 Fax: 0131 474 9292
Email: bob@cosla.gov.uk

Works to assist local authorities across Scotland to address and implement Local Agenda 21. Contact: Bob Christie, Local Agenda 21 Advisor.

Forward Scotland
6th Floor, Portcullis House, 21 India Street, Glasgow G1 4JH Tel: 0141 222 5600 Fax: 0141 222 5601
Email: forward.scotland@virgin.net

Forward Scotland works with a wide range of organisations to promote sustainable development through partnership projects, small grants and policy and research initiatives.

Friends of the Earth Scotland
72 Newhaven Road, Bonnington Mill, Edinburgh EH6 5QG Tel: 0131 554 9977 Fax: 0131 554 8656
Email: info@foe-scotland.org.uk
Website: www.foe-scotland.org.uk

FoE is a campaigning organisation, researching and publishing information on environmental issues, promoting the concept of sustainable development and a sustainable Scotland.

Islay Development Company (IDC)
Distillery Road, Port Ellen, Isle of Islay PA42 7AH
Tel: 01496 300 010 Fax: 01496 300 020
Email: info@islay.org.uk

IDC is owned by local people, who work with public and private organisations to implement sustainable development for the island.

Letslink Scotland
31 Banavie Road, Glasgow G11 5AW
Tel: 0141 339 3064 Email: pboase@gn.apc.org

Letslink Scotland is the umbrella organisation for Local Exchange Trading Schemes (LETS) in Scotland. It provides training and development for local groups and supports them by organising regional contacts and distributing information.

Recycling Advisory Group Scotland (RAGS)
5th Floor, Scott House, 10 South St Andrew Street, Edinburgh EH2 2AZ Tel: 0131 524 7049
Fax: 0131 557 3787 Email: RAGS2@compuserve.com

RAGS is a networking organisation promoting sustainable waste management in businesses and community groups and with individuals.

Scottish Borders Forum on Sustainable Development
c/o 19 Ferguson View, West Linton, Scottish Borders EH46 7DJ Tel: 01968 660678
Email: sbsfv@rsms.demon.co.uk
Website: www.rsms.demon.co.uk/forum.htm

A partnership of over 50 organisations and individuals with an interest, concern or responsibility for the environment in the Scottish Borders. Initiatives include promotion of household waste reduction and bioregional mapping – a technique to help local communities plot their sustainable future.

Scottish Environmental Education Council (SEEC)
c/o University of Stirling, Stirling FK9 4LA
Tel: 01786 467867 Fax: 01786 467864
Email: seec@stir.ac.uk

SEEC is a national voluntary organisation which promotes education for sustainable living and supports the network of Regional Environmental Education Forums.

Scottish Environment LINK
2 Grosvenor House, Shore Road, Perth PH2 8BD
Tel: 01738 630804 Fax: 01738 643290
Email: enquiries@scotlink.org

LINK is the liaison body for Scottish environmental sector voluntary organisations, providing a forum for information exchange, discussion and concerted action.

Scottish Natural Heritage (SNH)
Battleby, Redgorton, Perth PH1 3EW
Tel: 01738 627921 Fax: 01738 827411
Email: wwwteam@snh-wia.demon.co.uk
Website: www.snh.org.uk

SNH is a public body that works to secure and enhance Scotland's natural heritage, and supports social inclusion in environmental issues. It works at all levels, from conserving the countryside and promoting sustainable agriculture to supporting grassroots community projects in urban areas.

TRANSform Scotland
72 Newhaven Road, Bonnington Mill, Edinburgh EH6 5QG Tel: 0131 467 7714 Fax: 0131 554 8656
Email: campaigns@transformscotland.org.uk
Website: www.transformscotland.org.uk

A partnership of organisations who campaign for sustainable transport policies and practices in Scotland.

Northern Ireland

ARENA Network
c/o Business in the Community, 770 Upper Newtownards Road, Belfast BT16 0UL
Tel: 028 90410410 Fax: 028 90419030
Email: arena@bitc.org.uk
Website: www.greentriangle.arenani.org

ARENA Network is the Environmental Campaign of Business in the Community in Northern Ireland. It aims to ensure that progress towards Sustainable Development is an essential part of business excellence.

The Foyle Basin Council (FBC)
10 Clarendon Street, Derry BT48 7ET
Tel: 028 71377970 Fax: 028 71279706
Email: fbc@sustainableireland.org
Website: www.sustainableireland.org

The FBC is a non-governmental organisation promoting Local Agenda 21 and delivering training and advice to Derry City Council and local community organisations. The FBC is also involved in supporting Local Agenda 21 activity in the Republic of Ireland.

Northern Ireland Local Agenda 21 Advisory Group
c/o The Secretariat, Sustainable Northern Ireland Programme (as below)
Website: www.sustainableireland.org/advisory.htm

The Advisory Group was set up in January 1999 by the Northern Ireland Minister for the Environment and is composed of representatives from local authorities, the Department of the Environment in Northern Ireland, agriculture, business and the community and voluntary sector. The aim of the Group is to promote greater awareness of sustainable development in general and of Local Agenda 21 in particular and their relevance to key sectors in Northern Ireland.

Sustainable Northern Ireland Programme (SNIP)
75a Cregagh Road, Belfast BT6 8PY
Tel: 028 90507850 Fax: 028 9050785
Email: heather@snip1.freeserve.co.uk

SNIP works with local authorities and communities involved in Local Agenda 21 activities. Staff are involved in community participation work, indicators research and developing partnerships with community based organisations. SNIP was launched by the Northern Ireland Environment Link, a network environmental organisations.
Contact: Dr. Sue Christie, Tel. 028 90314944

Worldwide Fund for Nature (WWF)
11 West Street, Carrickfergus BT38 7AR
Tel: 01960 355166 Fax: 01960 355166
Email: jkitchen@wwfnet.org

WWF is one of the UK NGOs supporting Local Agenda 21 work in Northern Ireland. Core activities include campaigns on vanishing species, climate change, the UK countryside campaign and occasional workshops and seminars on sustainable communities.

Wales

Countryside Council for Wales (CCW)
Plas Penrhos, Penrhos Road, Bangor, Gwynedd LL57 2LQ Tel: 01248 385500 Fax: 01248 355782

Environment Agency Wales
Rivers House, St Mellons Business Park, St Mellons Cardiff CF3 0LT Tel: 029 20 770088 Fax: 029 20 798555
Website: www.environment-agency.wales.gov.uk

Groundwork Wales
Business Development Centre, Main Avenue, Treforest Industrial Estate, Treforest, Pontypridd CF37 5UR Tel: 01443 844866 Fax: 01443 844822
Email: gwtwales@globalnet.co.uk

Keep Wales Tidy Campaign
33–35 Cathedral Road, Cardiff CF1 9HB
Tel: 029 20 256767 Fax: 029 20 256768
Email: sandrah@tidybritain.org.uk

National Assembly Sustainable Development Unit
National Assembly for Wales, Cathays Park, Cardiff CF1 3NQ Tel: 029 20 823818 Fax: 029 20 825008
Email: lisa.dobbins@wales.gsi.gov.uk

The Prince's Trust – Cymru
4th Floor, Empire House, Mount Stuart Square, Cardiff CF10 5FN Tel: 029 20 471121 Fax: 029 20 482086
Email: pamthoma@princes-trust.org.uk

The Trust has played a leading role in voluntary sector work on sustainable development in Wales and can provide more detailed information.

Wales Council for Voluntary Action (WCVA)
Llys Ifor, Crescent Road, Caerphilly CF83 1XL
Tel: 029 20 855100 Fax: 029 20 855101
Website: www.wcva.org.uk

Wales Wildlife and Countryside Link
6a The Science Park, Aberystwyth, Ceredigion SY23 3AH Tel: 01970 611621 Fax: 01970 611621
Email: ruth@waleslink.demon.co.uk

Welsh Development Agency
Environment Director, QED Centre, Treforest Industrial Estate, Treforest, Pontypridd CF37 5YR
Tel: 01443 845513 Fax: 01443 845588
Email: tracy.stinchcombe@wda.co.uk

England

There are many organisations working locally on sustainable development issues in parts of England. A few are listed below.

Bioregional Development Group
The Ecology Centre, Honeywood Walk, Carshalton, Surrey SM5 3NX Tel: 020 8773 2322 Fax: 020 8643 6419

An innovative organisation working on a range of projects on sustainable use of the local natural environment and appropriate technology.

Environ
Parkfield, Western Park, Hinckley Road, Leicester
LE3 6HX Tel: 0116 285 6675 Fax: 0116 255 2343

Environ developed as the organisation running Leicester's Environment City programme and now offers consultancy services across the UK.

Southampton Environment Centre
Gracechurch House, 25–35 Castle Way, Southampton
SO14 2BW Tel: 028 80336172 Fax: 020 80336191
Email: la21@sec.gn.apc.org

One of a number of such centres around the UK, SEC works with local business on LA21 and has a community outreach programme.

Sustainable London Trust
7 Chamberlain Street, London NW1 8XB
Email: slt@gn.apc.org
Website: www.greenchannel.com/slt/index.htm,
also see: www.london21.org.

The Trust helps co-ordinate the London 21 sustainability network, has produced its own proposals for a more sustainable London, and has helped develop the London 21 website and database.

Sustainability North-West
The Environment Centre, Williamson Building, Oxford Road, Manchester M13 9PL Tel: 0161 275 7861
Fax: 0161 275 7865 Email: snw@snw.org.uk
Website: www.snw.org.uk

A new business-focused regional organisation that enourages business involvement in this work and is seeking to ensure that sustainability is built into the strategy of the NW Regional Development Agency.

West Midlands Environment Network (WMEN)
218 The Custard Factory, Gibb Street, Birmingham
B9 4AA Tel: 0121 772 5222 Fax: 0121 772 5444.
Email: wm.en@virgin.net

WMEN provides support for local organisations working on sustainability throughout the region and monitors the progress of LA21 initiatives.

UK21
c/o Projects in Partnership, 2nd floor,
The Tea Warehouse, 10a Lant Street, London SE1 1QR
Tel: 020 7407 8585 Fax: 020 7407 9555

UK21 is a developing independent network of locally-based organisations and individuals working to promote more sustainable communities.

Index of organisations

Action with Communities in Rural England (ACRE) 63
Advisory Committee on Business and the Environment (ACBE) 55, 71
Age Concern England 17, 59
Allotments Coalition Trust (ACT) 7, 32
Aluminium Can Recycling Association 22
ARENA Network 81
Association for Commuter Transport (ACT) 26
Association for the Conservation of Energy (ACE) 17
Association for Environment Conscious Building (AECB) 31
Association of Local Authorities in Northern Ireland (ALANI) 58

Baha'i Faith 76
Baratraria Foundation 37
Bat Conservation Trust 14
Bioregional Development Group 82
Black Environment Network (BEN) 48, 60
Breadline Britain 41
British Association for Fair Trade Shops 37
British Association of Settlements and Social Action Centres (BASSAC) 42, 63
British Glass 22
British Government Panel on Sustainable Development 55
British Plastics Federation 22
British Standards Institution (BSI) 71
British Trust for Conservation Volunteers (BTCV) 61, 66
British Youth Council 66
Building Research Establishment (BRE) 21, 31, 79
Business in the Community 37
Business in the Environment (BiE) 71
Butterfly Conservation 14

Cabinet Ministerial Committee on the Environment (ENV) 55
CAMPARIE 28
Carbon Storage Trust 17
Carsharing 28
Catholic Institute for International Relations (CIIR) 76
Centre for Alternative Technology (CAT) 17, 24, 31, 66, 79
Centre for Community Visions 46
Centre for Creative Communities 75
Centre for Sustainable Design 22
Centres for Change 63
CHANGE 65
Charity Logistics 37
Charter88 59
Child Poverty Action Group (CPAG) 39, 59
Christian Aid 61
Christian Ecology Link 76
Church Action on Poverty (CAP) 39, 59

Civic Trust 30
Common Ground 14, 33, 75, 79
Communities Against Toxics (CATs) 61
Community Action Network 43
Community Architecture Group 31
Community Car Share Network (CCSN) 26
Community Composting Network (CCN) 21
Community Development Foundation (CDF) 33, 39, 43, 46, 63, 79
Community Environment Resource Unit (CERU) 43
Community Links 43
Community Matters 43, 63, 64
Community Recycling Network (CRN) 21
Community Safety 12
Community Sector Coalition 63
Community Self-Build Scotland 80
Community Service Volunteers 59
Compassion in World Farming (CIWF) 7
Computer Recycling 21
Confederation of Indian Organisations (UK) 64
Construction Resources Centre 32
Consumers Association 59
Convention of Scottish Local Authorities (COSLA) 58, 81
Council for Environmental Education (CEE) 66, 69, 79
Council for the Protection of Rural England (CPRE) 9, 61
Countryside Council for Wales (CCW) 14, 82
Crime Concern 12
Crime Reduction Unit 12
CSV Environment (Scotland) 80
Cyclists' Touring Club (CTC) 26

Department of the Environment, Transport and the Regions (DETR) 24, 28, 50, 57
    Biodiversity Secretariat 15
Development Education Association 69
Development Trusts Association (DTA) 43, 64
'Doing Your Bit' 57
Don't Choke Britain 27
DTI-UK Eco-efficiency Initiative (UKEEI) 71

EarthRights Solicitors 48
Eco-Congregation – The Churches Environmental Project 76
Eco-Schools 66
Ecological Design Association 32
ELTIS 28
Empty Homes Agency 33
Energy Conservation & Solar Centre (ECSC) 17
Energy Efficiency Advice Centres 17
Energy Efficiency Best Practice Programme (EEBPP) 17, 71
Energy Efficiency Enquiries Bureau 28
Energy Saving Trust 18
Engender 65

English Nature 15
Entrust 22
Environ 83
Environment Agency 24, 50, 57
Environment Agency Wales 82
Environment Council 61
Environment and Energy Helpline 24
Environment Resource and Information Centre (ERIC) 58
Environment Trust 49
Environmental Action Fund 57
Environmental Audit Committee (EAC) 55
Environmental Law Foundation 50
Environmental Technology Support Unit (ETSU) 71
Environmental Transport Association (ETA) 27
Ethical Consumer Research Association (ECRA) 61
Ethical Investment Research Service (EIRIS) 37
Ethical Property Company plc (EPC) 72
European Anti-Poverty Network (EAPN) 39
European Anti-Poverty Network–England 40

Fair Shares 37
Farmers Market Help-line 8
Fawcett Society 65
Federation of City Farms and Community Gardens 8, 32, 64
Federation of Independent Advice Centres 59
Food and Drink Federation 8
Forum for the Future 37, 61, 72
Forward Scotland 81
Foundation for Community Dance 75
Foyle Basin Council (FBC) 82
Free Form Arts Trust 75
Friends of the Earth (England, Wales & Northern Ireland) 50, 61, 79
Friends of the Earth (FoE) 8, 15, 18, 21, 24, 27
Friends of the Earth Scotland 49, 61, 79, 81
Friends of the Western Buddhist Order 76
Furniture Recycling Network 21

Global Action Plan (GAP) 61
Going for Green 51, 57, 61, 69, 79
Green Alliance 61
Green Candle Dance Company 75
Green Ministers Committee 55
Greenpeace 61
Groundwork Foundation 32, 61, 67, 72, 79
Groundwork Wales 82

Heads Together 75
Health & Housing 5
Health for All Network (UK) 5
Health Education Authority 8
Help the Aged 40, 59
Henry Doubleday Research Association (HDRA) 8, 21
HLNET 6

ICOREC – Alliance of Religions and Conservation 76
Improvement and Development Agency (IDeA) (formerly Local Government Management Board) 15, 51, 79

Industry Council for Packaging and the Environment 22
Inter-Action Trust 43
International Society for Ecology and Culture (ISEC) 61
Islay Development Company (ICD) 81

Joseph Rowntree Foundation 34
Jubilee 2000 Coalition 37

Keep Wales Tidy Campaign 82

Landlife 15
Law Centres Federation 59
Learning Through Landscapes (LTL) 62
Letslink Scotland 81
LETSlink UK 37
Living Earth 67
Local Councils 18
Local Government Anti-Poverty Unit (LGAPU) 40
Local Government Association (LGA) 18, 58, 80
Local Government Management Board, see Improvement and Development Agency (IDeA)
Lothian Poverty Alliance 41
Low Pay Unit 40, 60

Magic Me 75
Marine Conservation Society 24
Mendip District Council 15
MIND – the National Association for Mental Health 60
Money Advice Association 60

National Alliance for the Care and Resettlement of Offenders (NACRO) 12
National Assembly Sustainable Development Unit 82
National Association of Citizens Advice Bureaux (NACAB) 40, 41, 60
National Association of Councils for Voluntary Service (NACVS) 60
National Association of Volunteer Bureaux 60
National Centre for Business and Ecology (NCBE) 72
National Centre for Volunteering 60
National Consumer Council (NCC) 60
National Council for Voluntary Organisations (NCVO) 49, 60
National Federation of Women's Institutes 65
National Recycling Forum 22
National Society for Clean Air and Environmental Protection (NSCA) 62
National Water Demand Management Centre 24
National Women's Network 65
Neighbourhood Energy Action (NEA) 18
Neighbourhood Initiatives Foundation (NIF) 33, 43
New Economics Foundation (NEF) 37, 62, 72, 80
Newham Council 67
NHS Executive 5
Northern Ireland Local Agenda 21 Advisory Group 82

Office of Electricity Regulation (Offer) 18
Oxfam 40, 41, 62, 65, 80

Panel on Sustainable Development 57
Pedestrians Association (PA) 27
Permaculture Association 8
Pesticides Trust 8
Pioneer Health Centre 5
Planning Aid for London 30
Plantlife – The Wild Plant Conservation Charity 15
Poverty Alliance 40
Primary Care Groups and Healthy Neighbourhoods 5
Prince of Wales Business Leaders Forum 72
Prince's Trust – Cymru 82
Projects in Partnership (PiP) 62

Quaker Peace and Service 76

Recycling Advisory Group Scotland (RAGS) 81
Rescue Mission: Planet Earth 67
Royal Association for Disability and Rehabilitation (RADAR) 60
Royal Commission on Environmental Pollution 55, 57
Royal Society for the Protection of Birds 8, 15
Royal Town Planning Institute (RTPI) 30

Safe Neighbourhoods Unit (SNU) 12
SALVO 22
Save the Children Fund 40, 62
Save Waste and Prosper (SWAP) 21
Scottish Borders Forum on Sustainable Development 81
Scottish Environment LINK 81
Scottish Environmental Education Council (SEEC) 81
Scottish Natural Heritage (SNH) 15, 81
Scottish Poverty Information Unit 41
Secretariat for Advisory Committee on Business and the Environment 57
Secretariat for Panel on Sustainable Development Education 57
Secretariat for Round Table 57
SERA 62
Shell Better Britain Campaign 32, 51, 62, 80
Shelter 32, 40
Sia: The National Development Agency for the Black Voluntary Sector 64
Social Venture Network Europe 72
Soil Association 8, 62
Solar Century 18
Sound Sense 75
Southampton Environment Centre 83
Standing Committee on Community Development (SCCD) 43
Standing Conference for Community Development 64
Steel Can Recycling Information Bureau 22
StudentForce for Sustainability 67
Surfers Against Sewage (SAS) 24
SUSTAIN – the Alliance for Better Food and Farming 8
Sustainability North-West 83

Sustainable Development Commission 55
Sustainable Development Education Panel 55
Sustainable Development Unit 57, 58
Sustainable London Trust 83
Sustainable Northern Ireland Programme (SNIP) 82
Sustrans 27

Tenants Participation Advisory Service for England (TPAS) 33, 46
The 1990 Trust 49
Tidy Britain Group 62
Town and Country Planning Association (TCPA) 30, 62
Trades Union Congress 74
Traffic Advisory Unit Driver Information & Traffic Management Division 26
Training and Enterprise Councils (TECs) 72
TRANSform Scotland 81
Transport 2000 (T2000) 27
TravelWise 27
Triodos Bank 72

UK21 83
UK Coalition Against Poverty 40
UK Public Health Association (UKPHA) 5
UK Round Table on Sustainable Development 55
UNIFEM-UK 65
United Nations Environment and Development – UK Committee (UNED–UK) 62, 65, 80
Urban Forum 30
Urban Wildlife Partnership (UWP) 32
URBED 33

Wages for Housework (WfH) 65
Wales Council for Voluntary Action (WCVA) 40, 82
Wales Wildlife and Countryside Link 82
Waste Watch 21, 22
Wastebusters Ltd 21
WATCH 67
Water UK 24
WaterAid 24
Welsh Anti-Poverty Network 40
Welsh Development Agency 82
West Midlands Environment Network (WMEN) 83
Wildlife Trusts (RSNC) 15, 62
Wind and Sun Ltd 18
Women's Design Service (WDS) 30
Women's Environmental Network (WEN) 21, 65
Women's National Commission 65
Woodcraft Folk 67
World Business Council for Sustainable Development 72
World Development Movement (WDM) 62
World Health Organisation 6
World Resource Foundation 21
World Wide Fund for Nature (WWF–UK) 9, 15, 62, 69, 80, 82

Youth Clubs UK 67